THE SUPERCONSCIOUS WORLD
PETER REVEEN

THE SUPERCONSCIOUS WORLD
PETER REVEEN

Eden Press
Montréal

THE SUPERCONSCIOUS WORLD
By Peter Reveen

ISBN: 0-920792-86-3

© 1987 Peter Reveen
First Edition. All rights reserved.
No part of this book may be reproduced, stored in a retrieval system, or transmitted in any form or by any means, electronic, mechanical, photocopying, recording, or otherwise, without the written permission of the publisher.

Cover design: EDDESIGN
Cover photograph: Larry Hanna
Inside page design: Lynette Stokes

Printed in Canada at Metropole Litho Inc.
Dépot légal — troisième trimestre 1987
Bibliothèque nationale du Quebec

Eden Press
31 A Westminster Avenue
Montreal, Quebec H4X 1Y8

Canadian Cataloguing in Publication Data

Reveen, Peter
 The superconscious world

Includes index.
ISBN 0-920792-86-3

1. Hypnotism.   2. Mental suggestion.   I. Title

BF1156.S8R48,1987   154.7   C87-090202-4

ACKNOWLEDGEMENT

I wish to express my indebtness to attorney Gary Ouellet, who not only wrote the introduction, but also drew my attention to a number of items I might otherwise have missed; psychiatrist and medical hypnotist Dr. Fred Kolough, who was reading the manuscript with the intention of writing a preface when he was unfortunately taken from us; and historian Dr. William Harwood who, when this project was first broached, spent many hours at Cambridge University and the British Library tracking down every source document I could possibly need, and more recently helped me edit several hundred first-draft pages down to the concise form you see here. To the many others who helped and encouraged me over the years, I also say thank you.

TABLE OF CONTENTS

INTRODUCTION
BY GARY Q. OUELLET, Q.C.
— 1 —

CHAPTER ONE
THE SUPERCONSCIOUS WATCHDOG
— 5 —

CHAPTER TWO
SUPERCONSCIOUS BEGINNINGS
— 18 —

CHAPTER THREE
ON MESMER'S COATTAILS
— 35 —

CHAPTER FOUR
SUPERCONSCIOUS HISTORY AFTER MESMER
— 52 —

CHAPTER FIVE
SUPERCONSCIOUS LIFE REGRESSION
— 70 —

CHAPTER SIX
**SUPERCONSCIOUS USES
AND ABUSES**
— 89 —

CHAPTER SEVEN
**A SUPERCONSCIOUS
TRAVELER'S TALES**
— 109 —

NOTES
— 126 —

INDEX
— 131 —

*Dedicated to Edith M. Hutchinson,
Coral, and the boys,
who always believed in me.*

INTRODUCTION

Until 1970, I had seen only one stage hypnotist, and was far from impressed. The fellow in question billed himself as The Great Richard, and was some kind of local low-life whose show was a glorified act of barbarism.

The Great Richard started by inviting volunteers on stage and hypnotizing them. They were then to regale the assembled fans by being made to eat candles and have pins and needles thrust through their cheeks. Interspersed with such elegant carryings-on, The Great Richard would plug his private sittings where, for a fee, he would transfer to the mark some of his "mindpower."

The ending surpassed all that had preceded it. Richard would announce to his volunteers that he was about to shoot them dead. He would then aim and fire a blank gun at each victim in turn. The loud reports of the gunfire were drowned by the louder cheers of the bloodthirsty audience who, it appeared, were all fans of Richard, and knew exactly what to expect.

I promised myself, never again. And then I started hearing tales of a fellow called Reveen, whose show was without equal. Friends who had seen Reveen urged me to travel any distance to see what they all universally described as the greatest show they had ever seen.

THE SUPERCONSCIOUS WORLD

One Saturday night in 1970, I drove one hundred and seventy-five miles with my wife-to-be, from Quebec City to Montreal, to witness this phenomenon. The show was everything promised, and more. We laughed. We screamed. We applauded. We gasped with amazement. Reveen displayed super memory feats, a sense of humor, and — especially — a magnificent sense of theater. As someone not unfamiliar with the field [1], I marvelled that here was a family show that had everything: humor, drama, and a heroic figure. For three hours on the return drive that night, there was only one subject of conversation: The Man They Call Reveen. For the next ten years, I only saw Reveen again through his occasional television appearances.

We were to meet in person through magic — we shared an interest in conjuring and illusion, and he had read some of my books on the subject — and that led to a professional association: I was eventually to become Reveen's legal advisor. This developed into a friendship where, today, we rarely miss a week without speaking to each other, and either Renee and I, or Reveen and Coral, visit each other or meet for a few days at some point on Reveen's many tours.

I have now seen the show dozens and dozens of times. I never get bored. I truly believe that the Reveen show is the best of its kind, and possibly the best of any kind. I bring my children to the show whenever I can. As a performer, his integrity is unequalled.

Reveen has played to more people live in Canada than any other entertainer in history. In Canadian theaters, his one-star show has just attained the six-million mark, a pretty remarkable figure. He has induced the superconscious state in tens of thousands of volunteers.

And I know of no one more qualified to debunk the mindbenders, to lay bare the scams of the channelers, mystics, and other psychological bunco men and women.

It is interesting that it is usually the professional performers who expose the frauds, not the scientific community, who are often gulled into belief along with the laity. It was Houdini who exposed the spiritualists and mediums of his time; it was the Amazing Randi who debunked Uri

THE SUPERCONSCIOUS WORLD

Geller; and it is Reveen who sets the record straight on hypnotism, mesmerism, channeling, reincarnation, and other curious claims.

It may have all started in 1963, when an Indian mystic, gaining fame with a product called "transcendental meditation," was knocking hypnotism in general and Reveen in particular. Reveen was invited by a television station in Calgary to come and join in the discussion. At the station, Reveen was escorted to the control booth where he was shown a tape of the eminent one's rantings. The guru was suggesting that only his meditational techniques could be an answer to the ills of the day. Reveen then entered the set. The moderator was Jim Butler. The guru was also on the set, in lotus position, sniffing flowers.

Reveen suggested that the mystic was perhaps ill-informed, that his comments suggested an attempt to gain cheap publicity for the guru's super scam. The guru giggled and warned that anyone going to Reveen's show would go mad, and start falling asleep all over the city (at that point Reveen had performed thirty-two concerts in the 1900-seat theater, and people were managing, with evident success, to keep awake from suburb to suburb!). The guru giggled some more, and said that Reveen was a "mere boy with a beard."

Reveen asked the mystic why people should be expected to pay hundreds of dollars for his teachings, when the same teachings could be found in hundreds of readily-available books on yoga and meditation. The guru, with an air of infinite patience, forgave Reveen for his transgressions and his ignorance. The holy one sniffed the flowers. When Reveen asked him why he carried around bouquets, the mystic replied that the flowers brought him serenity and kept away evil forces. He giggled some more, but in a noticeably higher key. Flowers or no flowers, the strain of direct questioning was beginning to tell.

The guru explained that, unlike Reveen's dangerous dropsy game, meditation could bring heaven to earth, — especially during the special seminar weekends at Banff at the guru's low, negotiated hotel rates, which he quoted and offered.

During the commercial break, Reveen sneaked out to make a few telephone calls. When the show resumed, Reveen suggested that Swami get a new business manager, because he was paying ten dollars more than the regular rate. This triggered a tirade against the "lying boy and his racket."

At the last commercial break, the floor director whispered in Reveen's ear that the producer would really appreciate it if Reveen could further prod the flower prince. Jim Butler then started hoping, on air, that there were no ill feelings between the two guests. The eminent one cackled, claimed he was a child of peace, and in a patently magnanimous act of human generosity, forgave the "ignorance of the boy." Reveen replied that he harbored no ill whatever, and, on the contrary, was always happy to meet a fellow showman.

That did it! Old man serenity started bouncing up and down on his goatskin like a possessed yo-yo, and his voice shot up still another octave as he shrilled "I am not a showman. I am not a showman." Flower petals were everywhere.

A few weeks later, Reveen was invited to participate in a further debate on CJAY TV in Winnipeg with the yogi. Reveen accepted, but the holy one did not show up. Baloney, William F. Buckley once noted, rejects the grinder. "I wish the Beatles could have seen the tape," says Reveen. "It could have saved them some money."

Perhaps the publication of this book will save us all some money. More importantly, it will answer important questions on subjects for which the most incredible claims are currently being made. For the most part, Reveen argues convincingly that the claims are *hocus pocus*.

Reading this has been a pleasant surprise, for I have discovered Reveen "the author," who has managed a difficult feat indeed: to take a well-researched document that qualifies, in many ways, as an academic contribution to the mind/cult and hypnotic corpus, and keep it an easy read, a fun read, and an interesting and compelling read.

Gary Q. Ouellet, Q.C.

[1] Mr. Ouellet, apart from his published writings, in both English and French, on law and politics, is also the author of a dozen books about conjuring.

CHAPTER ONE

THE SUPERCONSCIOUS WATCHDOG

As parties go, it was a success and proceeding smoothly. Gathered throughout the entertainment areas of the vast mansion were friends and colleagues of the genial host. He himself was moving from group to group, pausing to chat amiably or listen to the latest gossip. He was an eminent psychiatrist. By dispensing therapy to Hollywood's idle rich, he had become a famed pillar of the community, and his guests were the cream of Beverly Hills society.

He had married rich, and his wife's personal wealth contributed significantly to his opulent lifestyle. On this night, neither she nor their guests suspected that the apparently carefree host was in fact confronting a problem that threatened to bring both his standard of living and his career to an abrupt end.

Our doctor, it seems, had developed an intimate liaison with a patient, and she had issued an ultimatum that he legitimize their relationship by divorcing his wife, or she would expose him to one and all.

The doctor's dilemma solved itself, however, when, during the time he was busily entertaining his guests, the television news reported that his paramour had leaped to her death from the top floor of her high-rise apartment building on the other side of the city.

THE SUPERCONSCIOUS WORLD

At this point it should be revealed that our doctor was a skilled hypnotherapist, and had used hypnosis in the treatment of his late lamented patient. And, despite the fact that several witnesses had seen her leap to her death unassisted — the doctor had in fact murdered her.

"How so?" you justifiably ask. Simple. He had hypnotized her over the telephone!

It is a standard procedure in hypnotism to give a patient a code word that will cause him to re-enter a hypnotic "trance" on any future occasion. Our medical cad had slipped into the library for a couple of minutes, telephoned the victim at her apartment, uttered the code word, and thereby put her into a condition in which she was incapable of disbelieving any fantasy that he suggested. He then told her that she was very hot and wanted a swim in a pool that was just below her balcony. He hung up the phone and returned to his guests. The patient promptly changed into her swimsuit, stepped out on to the balcony and dived several floors to the concrete below.

The perfect murder? Not so. Unfortunately for our fiendish medico, the case was assigned to Lieutenant Columbo of the NBC police.

By this time it has probably occurred to you that you have been had. So were the millions of viewers who saw the murder just described on television, and believed that something of the sort could really happen.

The storyline used in the "Columbo" script was just one more re-telling of the mythological concept of hypnotism that has existed since the word was first coined by Dr. James Braid in 1843. Hypnotists are reputed to have the power to make their subjects believe anything they say, and purveyors of fiction have found it economically expedient to perpetuate that fantasy.

At the risk of upsetting the traditionalists and disappointing the sensationalists, I am obliged to blow apart the mythical cloak that surrounds hypnotism before proceeding any further, in order that my readers may better understand the more important aspects and possibilities that exist in reality.

THE SUPERCONSCIOUS WORLD

No subject of any suggestion technique can be compelled to do anything that goes against his personal concept of morality or which threatens his personal welfare. That prohibition is an absolute, and cannot be circumvented by creating a fantasy situation in which the taboo behaviour would be acceptable. A person in a state of hypnosis or superconsciousness (I will define the difference as we progress along) is not in any sense at the mercy of the operator, as is, for example, a patient under an anesthetic.

The truth is that a person will respond readily to suggestion only so long as his personal code of morality is not challenged. When that line is crossed, the part of the thinking processes that for convenience I call the "watchdog" takes over, and full conscious reasoning is restored.

An instance of a seemingly harmless suggestion that unintentionally contradicted a volunteer's belief occurred on my stage during a tour of Eastern Canada as recently as 1985. I had for some time felt uneasy over the growing claims for a technique used by some psychologists called "past lives therapy," the validity of which is certainly unestablished. I therefore decided to conduct some experiments on stage that would help my audience to evaluate for themselves the truth of such claims.

On this particular night, the volunteers were instructed to go back in their thoughts to a time before they were born. As expected, the majority of the volunteers did just that. (Their reason for doing so will be discussed in the relevant chapter.) One young lady, in spite of the fact that she had responded perfectly to all previous suggestions, opened her eyes, totally aware that she was on stage and nowhere else. Since she had been an ideal subject for all previous tests, I retained her on stage until the past–lives experiment was concluded. She again proved an ideal subject for the remainder of the show.

After the concert ended, curious as to why she had not responded to that particular suggestion, I asked her to come back and see me. She did so, and revealed that her religion rejected reincarnation as a heresy. In refusing even to dream that she had lived before, she graphically demonstrated my earlier point that no firmly–held moral value or belief can be compromised by suggestion.

THE SUPERCONSCIOUS WORLD

Not even the most innocuous suggestion can escape the watchdog's scrutiny. It is common practice for a hypnotherapist to instruct his patient that, "You hear no other sound but my voice," for the purpose of focusing the patient's mind in order to prevent extraneous sounds from interfering with the treatment. Yet even that simple a suggestion will be rejected if the patient sees it as incompatible with his best interests, as the following case illustrates.

A female patient was hypnotized by her doctor for the purpose of undergoing an abdominal operation without the aid of chemical anesthetics. The doctor told her that she could hear only his voice, and her failure to react to the voices of other persons present indicated that the suggestion had been accepted. Yet moments after the patient had indicated an inability to "hear" an attending nurse, her fiancé entered the hospital room and spoke to her and she answered him.

That the patient in this case was indeed influenced by suggestion is surely attested by the fact that the doctor proceeded with the surgery as originally planned, and the patient evinced no evidence of pain throughout the entire operation. Told afterwards of her response to her fiance's voice in defiance of the doctor's instruction, she concluded that, "Love is stronger than hypnotism."

A more scientific explanation would be that the mind is willing to remain apparently dormant in any situation that does not threaten the individual's own perception of his welfare. The watchdog portion of the thought processes will, however, override any suggestion when the person's best interests appear to dictate that it do so.

It is interesting to note that for more than fifty years hypnotists and psychologists have been voicing two different and contradictory theories as to what hypnotism can or cannot accomplish in the hands of the unscrupulous. To the general public they have parroted the glib generalization (without realizing that it is totally true!) that no hypnotized person will obey a suggestion that he would refuse to obey if he were awake. At the same time, in private discussions with colleagues and students they have boasted that, by creating an alternate reality that would legitimize the suggestion, a hypnotist could in fact make a subject commit a crime or immoral act. Actually, it is the glib generalization that is true and the private elaboration that is nothing more than self-titillating wishful thinking. According to believers of this "trade secret," not only are crimes of violence possible, but so also are sexual improprieties.

Nonsense!

A man with an abhorrence to violence could not be seduced across that threshold and induced to commit a violent act, no matter how plausible the reason for doing so might seem in the suggested scenario, any more than a woman with religious objections to reincarnation could be made to fantasize a past life. A person instructed to commit a crime would open his eyes in full awareness of what the architect of the fantasy was trying to do to him. And that, my reader, is not wishful thinking. It is the logical conclusion drawn from all competent observational data gathered since the heyday of Anton Mesmer two centuries ago.

While on the subject of hypnotism mythology, I wonder how many of you remember the advertisements that used to appear in pulp magazines, picturing a scantily-clad woman in an obviously helpless trance, while the headline above read, "Bend Others To Your Will By The Power Of Hypnotism." As the thousands who sent their hard-earned coin to the possessors of this secret art discovered to their regret, the hypnotic seduction so highly touted in fiction was a dismal failure in the real world. That observation is further borne out by the embarrassingly well-publicized cases in which a tiny minority of unethical (and misinformed) doctors, dentists, psychiatrists, and psychologists have been prosecuted for trying to prove otherwise.

I realize that I may appear repetitious in my emphatic restatement of the limitations of susceptibility to suggestion, but legends die hard, and for that reason I feel that a degree of "overkill" is justified.

I also realize that I am making authoritative statements for which I am here citing only a small amount of experimental evidence. However, I must point out that over thirty years of observations of tens of thousands of volunteers on my stage, volunteers from all walks of life and many different countries, as well as my experience in cooperating with medical practitioners throughout the world in therapeutic applications, along with countless comparative discussions with professionals whose opinions I respect, leave no doubt in my mind of the correctness of my conclusion that an individual's free agency cannot be subverted by suggestion. While in theory that conclusion could be clinically tested, in actuality, for all practical purposes it cannot.

Consider this: Could even the certainty that the subject would refuse, justify an attempt to program him to commit an act of violence? I think not, and I am not aware of any ethical practitioner of suggestion who would disagree with me. In any case, even an unscrupulous investigator would be deterred from conducting such an experiment by the fact that its results would be impossible to publish.

I have already referred to the portion of the thought processes that protects an individual from harmful suggestions, or even suggestions that he merely perceives as being harmful, as a watchdog. The time has come to explain what the watchdog is and how it works. Obviously it is not some kind of separate entity akin to Freud's "superego" and "id." If I were to suggest that it was, I would be offering metaphysical nonsense every bit as absurd as the analogous ideas of Freud.

We have all seen persons who can simultaneously conduct a conversation on one subject and write a letter on another. We have also known others so incapable of dividing their concentration that they cannot tie their shoe-laces and chew gum at the same time. Nobody would suggest that the person who can perform two simultaneous tasks that would each require another person's undivided concentration, has two minds or even two sub-minds. Rather, the individual is able to divide his concentration into unrelated directions.

Similarly, *all* persons' thought processes can be so divided that, even while a subject's observable concentration is focussed on the suggestion of a hypnotist, he is simultaneously engaged in another level of thinking that the hypnotist can neither reach nor deceive. This second level remains at all times fully aware of objective reality, and is fully capable of asserting itself if it sees an externally-suggested fantasy heading in an unacceptable direction. It is this second level of thinking, or perhaps I should say second focus, that acts as a watchdog, or censor, protecting the individual from any adverse consequences of the other focus's retreat into suggestibility. And the watchdog never sleeps. Even during normal dreaming, the watchdog will awaken the dreamer if the dream is causing terror or potential harm, as anyone who has ever awakened at the height of a nightmare is well aware.

Up to this point I have referred mainly to "hypnotism." Yet anyone who has seen my concert knows that I abandoned hypnotism theory some years ago in favor of superconscious psychology. What then is the difference? Is it semantic hair-splitting? Just what is superconsciousness if it is not hypnotism?

We can start by asking "What is hypnotism?" The answer is that *hypnotism*, like every word in English or any other language, is whatever the persons using the word or hearing it understand it to be. Hypnotism has come to mean all of the things that two centuries of researchers, apologists and detractors have proclaimed, imagined, feared, hoped or suspected it to mean. Hypnotism is believed to be, and therefore *is*, a "power" in which one mind is dominated, subjugated and controlled by another. Hypnotism is an art and a science. Hypnotism is a power that can be used for evil as readily as for good. Hypnotism tampers with the mind. Hypnotism in the hands of the unskilled can do intentional harm or, just as easily, unintentional harm. Hypnotism is the work of the devil. Hypnotism is chemically-induced madness. Hypnotism is a hoax, a mountebank's trick. The definitions could be compounded *ad infinitum*. It therefore seems to me that, since the neo-occult "power" that is, by definition, hypnotism, does not exist, then we must logically conclude that hypnotism, as so defined, does not exist.

And yet a goodly portion of the observable phenomena once equated with hypnotism *does* exist. When the difference between the legitimate manifestations that *I* thought of as hypnotism, and the superstitious nonsense that the public at large accepted as hypnotism, began to bother me, my initial reaction was to try to counter the nonsense by appearing on as many radio and television shows as possible in order to educate the public as to the factual situation. But I realized that serious scholars have been trying to do that for more than a century with a conspicuous lack of success.

I had also begun to recognize that the trance or sleep theory behind hypnotism was at best an oversimplification, a failure to observe that a subject's apparent trance was as much a conditioned response to an induced fantasy as anything else he did at the hypnotist's suggestion. And this archaic "trance" concept also added fuel to the "power control" school of thought.

The only practical solution was to acknowledge that hypnotism meant a nonexistent occult power, and to coin a new and more accurate name for the latent mental abilities which do exist. Since volunteers on my stage continually displayed heightened capacities to perform usual and unusual tasks, capacities that often greatly exceeded those of normal consciousness, I needed a word that described minds more in control of their own destinies than in normal consciousness, in contrast to "hypnotism" which implied the precise opposite. It logically followed that, if a person capable of normal waking activities was "conscious," then a person in a state with greater capacities was "superconscious."

And that brings us back to my earlier question, "So what is the superconscious state?" It is not sleep, although the condition of total relaxation with the eyes closed has an external resemblance to sleep. It was that resemblance to sleep that led Dr. James Braid in the nineteenth century to coin the word *hypnosis,* from the Greek work *hypnos,* "sleep." Yet within a few years Braid himself recognized his error and tried to rename the condition he now realized was not sleep, "neurypnology," and still later, "monoideaism." By that time, however, the words hypnosis and hypnotism had become so widely sensationalized that Braid's attempt to abolish them as misleading failed.

Electro encephalograms have shown that brainwave patterns of superconscious subjects more closely resemble the waking than the normal sleeping pattern. This is consistent with my earlier conclusion that the mind's watchdog remains wide awake guarding the subject's physical and moral wellbeing. Just as a dreamer's rapid eye movements indicate a mind that is not inactive, so a superconscious subject's EEG patterns indicate a mind that is not asleep.

Some researchers in the past have described superconsciousness (although they used the word hypnotism) as an altered state of consciousness; but even that conservative definition has not been borne out by any physiological monitoring. If brain, heart, respiration, and other

THE SUPERCONSCIOUS WORLD

patterns remain unchanged during superconsciousness, whereas they do change during sleep, meditation or coma, then in what measurable way has the consciousness been altered? The answer would seem to be: none.

The one definition least likely to be challenged is that superconsciousness is a state of heightened suggestibility. That means that, within identifiable limits, a person who is superconscious is more likely to believe and act upon what he is told — even when what he is told is creatively beyond his normal personality pattern — than if he were merely conscious. A subject on my stage is observably in a state of heightened suggestibility. But as Vance Packard explains in *The Hidden Persuaders*, so is a person watching a subliminal message implanted into a television program.

A TV viewer can watch a commercial for a national brand of soft drink for thirty seconds and not feel compelled to go to the refrigerator in search of the advertised product. Yet he *is* compelled to do so by a slide that is flashed on the screen for so short a time, one twenty-fourth of a second, that he has no conscious awareness of seeing it. Clearly his mind has been rendered hyper-receptive — or suggestible — or superconscious, even though no condition remotely resembling sleep has been induced.

Superconsciousness is a state of heightened suggestibility. But it is observably much more than that. No student of history can dispute that the mobs which stood enraptured as they listened to the hate-mongering harangues of recent and not-so-recent dictators were in a state of heightened suggestibility. Had each individual member of the mob been removed from the emotion-charged atmosphere and quietly instructed to commit physical violence against a member of a minority group, an overwhelming majority would have refused. But because the individual's capacity to believe and obey whatever his leader uttered was heightened and reinforced by the observable adulation of thousands of others, his mind was opened to suggestions that would normally have been rejected as incompatible with his self-image.

The mobs were hyper-suggestible; but they were not superconscious. Had they been so, their leaders could have instructed them to look up and see legions in full battle array ready to lead them against their imagined enemies. And as mentally dysfunctional as the most powerful dictators undoubtedly were, none was capable of imagining for one second that he could do *that*.

So superconsciousness is more than just heightened suggestibility. It goes beyond that to the point where the body's senses, abilities and even autonomic systems are able to accept and respond to non-threatening hallucinations created by an external operator. A superconscious subject will not merely go through the motions of playing a non-existent piano when told to do so; he will actually see, feel and hear the piano as fully and realistically as in a non-induced dream.

Yet to a skeptic, what does the sight of a man or woman making piano-playing motions in empty space really prove? As recently as 1981, author Ian Wilson was able to write, "From the medical standpoint, to this day there is no known method for determining whether the state of hypnosis i.e., superconsciousness even exists,"[1] and that observation remains true today. Even a thousand subjects signing affidavits that they physically experienced the suggested piano, would not constitute objective proof that they had done so. And on the issue of suggested hallucinations, for most such suggestions no method of testing or measuring the reality of the hallucinations ever will exist.

Fortunately for science, however, the reality of a small but significant proportion of externally suggested superconscious fantasies can be and has been tested. Since most of my own experimentation in this area has been confined to stimulating latent artistic talent in my volunteers for the purpose of entertaining a theater audience, the cases I shall cite will be from the published work of others.

Dr. S.J. Van Pelt, longtime President of the British Society of Medical Hypnotists and editor of the Society's *Journal,* reports some interesting tests on the ability of a superconscious subject to vary his heart rate.[2] In the first test the subject's heart rate was measured and found to be a healthy 78. He was then told, while superconscious, that he was riding in an automobile and that a near-accident was occuring. His heart rate rose measurably.

THE SUPERCONSCIOUS WORLD

In the second test, a subject who also had a heart rate of 78 at the beginning of the experiment was, without being given any reason for it to do so, informed that his heart rate was starting to accelerate. He responded to the superconscious suggestion, and at the height of the experiment his heart rate had climbed to 135.

In a case first described by psychiatrist Morton Schatzman in *The Story of Ruth*,[3] and later cited by Ian Wilson,[4] a woman came to Dr. Schatzman suffering from terrifying hallucinations. Schatzman, recognizing the superconscious nature of hallucinations, was able to teach the patient, whom he gave the pseudonym of "Ruth," to hallucinate at will. He was thus enabled to test whether the hallucinated object triggered the same physical effects as it would if the fantasy had been real.

It must be noted that, even though Dr. Schatzman did not follow the common format of suggesting an alternate reality, the effect was the same as if he had done so. He did not say to Ruth, "I am turning on the light," but rather something along the lines of, "I want you to imagine you see me turning on the light." As Wilson described this first experiment:

> Her eyes showed nothing of the retinal change that would occur if a real light was switched on. She was unable to read by this hallucinated light the title of a book handed to her.

The preliminary experiment provided no objective evidence that the superconscious state exists. Further tests, however, were to produce a much more meaningful result.

In an experiment conducted by Schatzman and neurophysiologist Dr. Peter Fenwick at London's St. Thomas Hospital, electrodes were attached to Ruth's scalp in order to relay her brainwave patterns to an oscilloscope. She was then instructed to look at a television screen on which appeared a checkerboard whose squares changed color every second or so. As soon as the oscilloscope registered a discernible pattern, Ruth was instructed to hallucinate her daughter sitting on her knee and obstructing her view of the screen:

Immediately the oscilloscope's pattern changed, just as it would if a real person had come between Ruth and the screen. The experiment was repeated with several variations, always with the same result. Scientifically, the oscilloscope was confirming that Ruth was quite genuinely seeing in her mind that which all along she claimed to see, even though the vision had absolutely no reality.

Ruth, in a state of self-induced superconsciousness, saw, heard, felt and smelled persons who were not there. Once she had learned to trigger such hallucinations at will, she was able to accept that the "ghosts" that had initially terrified her into seeking psychiatric help were also generated by her own mind. With that realization, her problem was cured. She had seen her last ghost.

It is not my purpose to disabuse persons who choose to believe in ghosts. But it does seem obvious that, if one person who habitually saw ghosts could stop doing so after learning to control her tendency to create superconscious illusions, then all ghosts seen by a single individual in the presence of persons who could *not* see them can be similarly explained.

The mind's demonstrated ability to vary its brainwave patterns to accord with the presence or absence of a superconscious visual illusion, is the strongest objective evidence that the superconscious state is measurably real. But almost as strong is the ability of a superconscious patient to achieve the condition of total anesthesia necessary for the performance of major operations.

The earliest recorded use of what was currently being called "mesmerism" to induce anesthesia, ocurred in the field of dentistry. The year was 1837, and the practitioner who reported the successful use of superconsciousness for this purpose was Dr. Oudet in France. And in that same year a French "mesmerist" visited England and taught the technique to Dr. Elliotson, who used it for both healing and surgical anesthesia. Then shortly after that Dr. James Esdaile performed numerous operations on patients whom he had rendered superconsciously anesthetic. This method of simplifying operations continued to be used by Broca, Follin and others into the 1860s, the decade in which Guerineau amputated a leg under what had by then come to be called hypnosis.[5]

THE SUPERCONSCIOUS WORLD

The use of the superconscious state for painless operations fell considerably from favor following the development of such chemical anesthetics as nitrous oxide in 1844, ether in 1846 and chloroform in 1847. Today superconsciously-induced anesthesia as a substitute for chemical anesthetics is all but non-existent. Almost the only exceptions are those cases where a patient has an allergy to known anesthetics, and even then the use of superconsciousness is viewed as a novelty.[6]

Despite the clear evidence of painless operations, practitioners of superconsciousness continued to be labelled as quacks, charlatons, liars, and dupes long after the death of Anton Mesmer. While nobody dared label Esdaile a liar, they were not slow to pin such a label on his superconscious patients. Esdaile's 1856 response to his detractors remains as valid today as it was 130 years ago. For while Esdaile conceded that he had only his patients' own assurances that they felt no pain, it seemed to him that the allegation that hundreds of patients would allow him to perform complicated arm and leg amputations while merely pretending to feel no pain, for the dubious pleasure of deceiving him, was utterly ludicrous.

And so it seems to me.

CHAPTER TWO

SUPERCONSCIOUS BEGINNINGS

Something akin to superconscious suggestion appears to have existed from ancient times. Classical references to the "Druid sleep" immediately conjure up images of a druid priest using some kind of ritualistic chant, although he would not have recognized it as pure suggestion, to put ailing patients to "sleep" so that he could perform painless surgery or cure (non-viral) illnesses. Similar inferences can be drawn from Egyptian papyri and Greek documents relating to the school of Asklepios, as well as the building of "sleep" temples that seem to have spread right throughout Asia Minor.

Such inferences are at best tenuous. It seems most unlikely that a medical procedure that worked could have been lost for more than a thousand years. One has only to look at those "old wives' remedies" that survived to become the basis for successful drugs, and those that proved to be merely a focus for suggestion and continue to be used in that capacity, to see the improbability of a form of superconscious induction being discovered, lost for centuries, and rediscovered in the eighteenth century.

On the other hand, the use of suggestion to cure the mind of delusions is much more thoroughly documented.

As far back as the time of the Trojan War, *circa* 1250 BC, the Greeks believed that the body of a mortal could be "possessed" by a god for the purpose of enabling the god to perform physical acts, most commonly seduction but quite often heroic deeds such as participation in a war. By Homer's day, *c* 800 BC, the beliefs of Ionian Greeks had changed to the point where the gods had acquired their own physical bodies and the "possession" belief, being no longer necessary, had disappeared. Thus in the *Iliad* we find Aphrodite rescuing the injured Paris by carrying him in her arms, rather than "possessing" him bodily as she would have done in the pre-Homeric version of the eighth-century editor's source.

In citing Greek beliefs of the Heroic period, I am showing that belief in "possession" existed more than a thousand years before the idea arose that the immortals doing the possessing were necessarily malevolent. Only when the concept of possession was revived in Roman times were persons manifesting "possession" symptoms viewed as victims of evil demons and therefore in need of exorcism, or as we would say today, curing. Before proceeding to the role of suggestion in exorcisms there is something I must make clear. The reality of "possession" is not a belief of any modern religion. In labelling "possession" as a delusion curable by suggestion, I am therefore not challenging the right of any person to believe the teachings of his faith. Rather, I am simply putting an archaic belief into a coherent historical perspective.

The Greeks had stopped believing in possession by the eighth century BC. But the belief itself did not disappear. It was borrowed from the Ionian Greeks of what is now western Turkey by cultures centred farther east and preserved by them until some time after the victories of Alexander the Great, at which time it was passed on to the inhabitants of the Roman province of Judaea.

About two thousand years ago it was by no means uncommon for persons on the eastern coast of the Mediterranean to imagine themselves "possessed" by demons. Because delusions of any nature flourish only in an atmosphere of total credulity, and skepticism of alleged paranormal phenomena will invariably prevent its manifestation, no cases of possession were ever reported in Judaic communities outside of Judaea, or in such cosmopolitan communities within Judaea as Tyre and Caesaria. Possession was therefore not a "Jewish" belief, or even a geographically Judaic one.

THE SUPERCONSCIOUS WORLD

Nonetheless, within the confines of Judaea, persons who manifested symptoms of "possession" were rife — and, true to the law of supply and demand, so were exorcists, persons we can now identify as practitioners of superconscious suggestion to cure the victims' delusions. Since hundreds, even thousands of demons, immortal by definition, could not have ceased to exist in the intervening two thousand years, the total absence today of the kind of demon that can "possess" a mortal would seem clear evidence that such demons never did exist. That being so, the identification of exorcism as the unwitting use of superconscious suggestion seems fully justified. However, since such an interpretation does raise theological questions, and I am not a theologian, conclusions based solely on empirical historical data may well be challenged by persons who consider themselves more qualified in theological areas. That is their privilege. And since the proper superconscious technique for curing possession-delusion is to talk directly to the non-existent demon — in the hearing of the victim, obviously — we cannot infer that any ancient exorcist who used such a technique was necessarily unaware of the demons' non-existence.

General belief in demon-possession had disappeared from Europe by medieval times, only to be replaced by the equally mind-crippling absurdity of witchcraft. Just as a superconscious subject's belief that I (on stage) can render him dormant with an imaginary dart from a non-existent tranquilizer gun enables me to do so, so a medieval peasant girl's belief that a "witch" (usually any woman who had outlived her teeth) could make her ill by casting a "spell" enabled such an illness to occur whenever the victim was informed or imagined that such a spell had been cast. The superconscious nature of such illnesses, clearly revealed by the victim's need to learn of the alleged spell before it could take effect, is further attested by the fact that the symptoms disappeared whenever the victim was assured that the spell had been broken or withdrawn.

Note that the watchdog could not protect the victim of a possession- or bewitched-fantasy in a culture in which the entire thought processes had been culturally conditioned to believe in the reality of the fantasy. The watchdog cannot detect the discrepancy between reality and fantasy when the watchdog itself believes in the reality of the fantasy. The effects and techniques of cultural conditioning, Pavlovian conditioning, operant conditioning and brainwashing would take another book to explain, and in any case the definitive works on the subject have already been written:

THE SUPERCONSCIOUS WORLD

The Battle for the Mind by William Sargant,[1] and the relevant treatises of B.F. Skinner.

Exorcists used superconscious suggestion to cure victims of possession-delusion two thousand years ago. Priests and self-styled witches used superconscious suggestion to cure or inflict victims of enchantment-delusion five hundred years ago. Does that mean that the human mind's superconscious potential was at least dimly recognized if misperceived centuries before the experiments of Franz Anton Mesmer? It does not.

Only through hindsight are we able to recognize exorcisms and spell-breakings as superconscious talk-therapy. The exorcists tended to use the technique of talking to the demons they were exorcising precisely because they believed in the reality of the demons' existence. Priests who waved amulets and sprinkled holy water to combat the effects of witches, were quite convinced that harmless old women had unleashed a satanic force to wreak evil and that the consecrated paraphernalia ritually used was itself the source of any cure. The role of suggestion was never suspected.

Possession-delusion is dead. Bewitchment-delusion is dead. Unfortunately, similar culturally-conditioned delusions that can only be cured by disguised superconscious suggestion are alive and well and *not* hiding in Argentina. Consider the recent phenomenon of multiple personality.

Just as exorcists cured possession-delusions by talking directly to the non-existent demons, so modern psychotherapists attempt to cure multiple-personality-delusions by addressing their talk-therapy, not to the patient, but to the "other personality" inhabiting the patient's body. "Multiple personality" became the fashionable new "possession" craze with the publication of the book, *The Three Faces of Eve*, written by a therapist who believed in the reality of the intruding personalities as surely as any exorcist believed in the reality of the intruding demons. The release of a subsequent film triggered an epidemic of copycat cases, and now psychiatrists are rushing into print in a frantic display of psychological one-upmanship to claim the detection of ten, twenty or even more personalities in the one body. I cannot help but notice that the multiplication of personalities increases in direct proportion to the amount of published books, movies and television programs on the subject to which the patients have been exposed. While no doubt some psychiatrists talk directly to a fantasized personality in full awareness that this is the most effective superconscious technique, it seems certain that most persons who talk to non-existent personalities do so for the same reason exorcists talked to non-existent demons: chronic, unquestioning credulity.

The man who is rightly hailed as the father of modern superconscious talk-therapy was Franz Anton Mesmer (1734-1815). Like the exorcists, Mesmer used talk-therapy in the belief that he was doing something entirely different, for he believed that he was redirecting a very real magnetic fluid to correct a magnetic imbalance. What then was the difference between Mesmer and the exorcists? The answer is that Mesmer was the first person to recognize that he had detected and could manipulate a hitherto-unknown capacity of the human organism, and that he was not invoking the intervention of an external metaphysical healer. That Mesmer failed to realize that the capacity he had uncovered was suggestibility, but rather thought it was a magnetic fluid that permeates all living things, in no way lessens the enormous magnitude of what he discovered. Mesmer showed the world how to induce superconsciousness, and how to utilize the condition that he called "magnetic sleep" to effect a large variety of beneficial changes in the human body. It remained only for later researchers to ascertain the true nature of Mesmer's discovery.

Mesmer had no forerunners and he did not knowingly elaborate on or utilize the theories of others. His theory of animal magnetism did, however, parallel some of the writings of Paracelsus. Also, after Mesmer and a Jesuit, Father Hell, had worked together on a therapeutic methodology utilizing magnets, each claimed afterwards that it was he who had taught the technique to the other.

Paracelsus was born in Switzerland, not far from Zurich, in 1493. His family name was Phillipus Aureolus Theophrastus Bombastus von Hohenheim, and he was also sometimes referred to by other names, but he is best remembered as Paracelsus. He was a prolific traveller, and is thought to have been the first westerner to bring back and publish many of the beliefs of the Orient. According to his earliest biographer:[2]

> Every reader of the works of Paracelsus who is also acquainted with the recent revelations made by the Eastern Adepts, cannot fail to notice the similarity of the two

systems, which in many respects are almost identical, and it is therefore quite probable that Paracelsus during his captivity in Tartary was instructed in the secret doctrine by the teachers of occultism in the East. The information given by Paracelsus in regard to the sevenfold principles of man, the qualities of the astral body, the earth-bound elementaries, etc., was then entirely unknown in the West; but his information is almost the same as the one given in "Isis Unveiled," "Esoteric Buddhism," and other books recently published, and declared to have been given by some Eastern Adepts.

Paracelsus was described by Hartmann as "a Christian" who "always attempted to support the doctrines he taught by citations from the Bible."[3] Living as he did in a culture that contemplated burning Copernicus and Galileo for daring to suggest that the earth orbits the sun, Paracelsus' stressing of his religious orthodoxy could have been prudent expedience. Much of what he wrote had the potential to arouse the Inquisition's ire, so that finding biblical support for his theories was a logical safety play. Certainly his published opinion of contemporary medicine would have won him powerful enemies, and that alone would have encouraged him to seek all the ecclesiastical support he could get:[4]

> The best of our popular physicians are the ones that do the least harm. But, unfortunately, some poison their patients with mercury, others purge them or bleed them to death. There are some who have learned so much that their learning has driven out all their common sense, and there are others who care a great deal more for their own profit than for the health of the patients.

As Groucho Marx might have said, "So what else is new?"

On the subject of magnetism, Paracelsus wrote:[5]

> The sidereal man is of a magnetic nature, and for that reason he may attract the powers and effluvia of the astral world . . . . Man possesses a magnetic power by which he may attract certain effluvia of a good or evil quality

in the same manner as a magnet will attract particles of iron. A magnet may be prepared out of some vital substance that will attract vitality. . . . Such substances as the hair, the excrement, urine, blood, etc. . . . The Archaeus is an essence that is equally distributed in all parts of the human body . . . . The Archaeus is of a magnetic nature, and attracts or repulses other sympathetic or antipathetic forces belonging to the same plane . . . . The Archaeus is the essence of life, but the principle in which this essence is contained and which serves as its vehicle, is called Mumia . . . . The Mumia may act from one living being directly upon another . . . . The cures that have been performed by the use of the Mumia are natural, although they are very little understood by the vulgar.

The foregoing indeed parallels and foreshadows the explanation of his discoveries propounded by Mesmer, and Hartmann can hardly be blamed for concluding that, "Paracelsus, not Mesmer, is the original discoverer of so-called Mesmerism." [6] But Mesmer utilized a technique of suggestion that worked *despite* Mesmer's own belief in a magnetic fluid. Paracelsus, on the other hand, merely formulated a theory that is now known to be utterly false. What really led Hartmann to credit Paracelsus with the discovery of Mesmerism was his uncompromising adherence to the Paracelsus-Mesmer "magnetism" theory a full fifty years after Bertrand, Faria, Braid and others had given the world clear evidence that Mesmer's results were achieved by suggestion, not magnetism. At a time when more open-minded scholars knew better, Hartmann could still claim that, "Paracelsus was well acquainted with the therapeutic powers of the magnet, and used it in various diseases . . . . The knowledge of the therapeutic use of the magnet has not advanced much since the days of Paracelsus." [7]

Paracelsus propounded a theory of animal magnetism, and two centuries later Anton Mesmer explained his manipulation of the superconscious state by a theory of animal magnetism. But Paracelsus had written that, just as a magnet to influence iron particles needed to be made of iron, so a magnet to influence humankind's "vital substances" needed to be made out of material that had been in the body long enough to have accumulated some of its vitality. It seems evident that, if Mesmer had borrowed his theories from Paracelsus, he would have used magnets constructed on Paracelsus' principles. In fact the only magnets Mesmer ever used were made of iron.

On the question of whether Mesmer learned Paracelsian techniques and theories from Father Hell, the evidence is too ambiguous to justify my presenting a personal conclusion as if it were established fact. I will therefore quote first a writer who believes that he did, and then Mesmer's own words to the contrary, and let the reader decide for himself.

According to A.R.G. Owen:[8]

> For some years Mesmer worked in Vienna as a physician in general practice.... This brought him into contact with the Austrian Court Astronomer, Maximilian Hell, a Jesuit Father who was interested in Paracelsian type theories and was a magnet-therapist. Mesmer assisted in treatments with magnetized "tractors," iron plates attached to the patients, but he soon launched into his own experiments. He replaced the magnet and traction by his own system, including the fixed gaze and "passes."

Mesmer's account of his dealings with Father Hell is as follows:[9]

> My social relations with Father Hell, Jesuit and professor of astronomy at Vienna, then provided me with an opportunity of asking him to have made for me by his craftsmen a number of magnetised pieces, of convenient shape for application. He was kind enough to do this for me and let me have them.... I found out not too long afterwards, from the public and from the newspapers, that this man of religion, abusing his fame in astronomy and wishing to appropriate for himself a discovery of whose nature and benefits he was entirely ignorant, had taken upon himself to publish the fact that by means of some magnetised pieces, to which he attributed a specific virtue depending on their shape, he had obtained the means of curing the gravest nerve disorders.... And by affecting to confuse the manufacture of the magnetised shapes with

the discovery I had mentioned to him, he finished by saying, "that he had communicated everything to the physicians, and particularly to myself, and would continue to avail himself of them for his tests" . . . . The desire to refute such errors once and for all, and to do justice to truth, determined me to make no further use of electricity or of the magnet from 1776 onwards.

Anton Mesmer was not merely a link in the chain of discoverers from the unwitting users of superconscious suggestion two thousand years ago to its informed users of today. He was an innovator, the man who first recognized that there exists some kind of innate capacity of the human organism capable of being utilized and manipulated to cure bodily ills. During his lifetime and for many years afterwards he was the victim of much bad press. Even today Mesmer continues to be upbraided for misinterpreting the true nature of his discovery — usually by the same people who praise Columbus for discovering America and ignore his assertion to his dying day that he had reached India.

Mesmer was born in 1743, married in 1768, and died in 1815. He was far more educated than his detractors like to admit. D.M. Walmsley reports that,[10] "He mastered wide knowledge in science and arts at three universities before taking his doctorate in medicine with highest honors at Vienna |in 1766|."

Mesmer's academic distinction is often ignored, and undue attention focussed on the *title* of his doctoral thesis, "The Influence of the Planets on the Human Body." In fact Mesmer concluded that astrology, "which professed to foretell the future and thereby cheated its victims," is fraudulent. His research was rather into the nature of purely physical influences on living bodies, and stemmed directly from Newton's discovery that massive bodies do exert influence in the form of gravity. In 1766 research into the question of what, if any, other influence was exerted by planets was by no means unwarranted.[11]

It was in 1774 that Mesmer first attempted to utilize an "animal magnetism" theory he had formulated a decade earlier, to treat a patient who had failed to respond to current medical orthodoxy. He published an account of the case, including his revolutionary new treatment and the theory behind it, in 1775.

Mesmer's patient was a young woman named Franzl Oesterling. He described their first encounters as follows:[12]

> In my house a young woman of twenty-eight years who had suffered from nervous debility from her youth was attacked by terrible convulsions off and on for about two years. Her hysterical fever caused continual vomiting, inflammation of the bowels, stoppage of urine, excruciating toothache, earache, melancholy depression, delirium fits of frenzy, catalepsy, fainting fits, blindness, breathlessness, lameness, lasting some days, and other horrible symptoms. I applied with the utmost care the most efficacious remedies known, not leaving her out of my sight, frequently rescuing her from death's door; and I usually restored her within three weeks. But her recovery did not last long before she fell ill again into the same condition.

As a letter written by Leopold Mozart (father of Wolfgang Amadeus) makes clear, Mesmer's "efficacious remedies" included bloodletting, blistering and various medicines.[13] That they appeared to give temporary relief can be attributed to the placebo effect. To this day many doctors prescribe colored sugar pills for patients whose maladies they diagnose as psychosomatic, often with satisfactory results.

Franzl could have been cured by her own belief in the validity of a doctor's treatment. However, her chronic need to be an invalid always induced a prompt recurrence. What was needed to cure her permanently was the induction of a new belief, a belief in a new and revolutionary treatment that would make her famous as the first patient cured by such a method.

Mesmer did not realize that, of course. When he formed the intent to try to cure her through the use of magnets, he genuinely believed that he was harnessing a magnetic quality of the human organism. That he was curing his patient by *suggesting* that he was curing her did not cross his mind.

Writing of his decision to try magnetism, Mesmer declared:[14]

> I never gave up close observation of my patient in accordance with my theory, and became so involved that I experienced the condition myself, in the rise and fall of the illness. In the end I came to the conclusion that the ebb and flow in the body of the sick person was similar to those of magnets.

Satisfied that his magnetism theory at least merited testing, Mesmer proceeded with his plan:[15]

> In the month of July when my patient had another attack I fixed two magnets of horse-shoe type to her feet and a heart-shape magnet on her breast. Suddenly she felt a burning sensation spreading from her feet through all her joints like a glowing coal, with severe pains at the hips, and likewise from both sides of the breast to the crown of the head. It continued throughout the night, causing copious sweating .... the pains gradually went off, she became insensitive to the magnets. The symptoms disappeared and she recovered from the seizure.

By inducing in his patient a belief in a form of therapy that we now recognize as the unwitting use of suggestion, Mesmer triggered an emotional and physical upheaval that, after only two more attacks, was followed by a permanent cure. One cannot help but notice the similarity between that and some modern fringe cults that encourage believers to experience seizures in which they emit wolf howls and give long speeches in gibberish prior to acceptance into the cult.

Mesmer was as impressed by his patient's intense convulsions during this first treatment as by her subsequent cure, and he incorporated into his theory the necessity of bringing on a "crisis" before any cure could be effected. Modern therapists, familiar with the true capacity of the superconscious, tend to regard such crises as highly undesirable, and even the earliest generation of mesmerists departed from their founder's teaching on this point.

THE SUPERCONSCIOUS WORLD

Yet Mesmer was at least partly right. In the case of the most chronic illnesses not attributable to chemical imbalance, cure by normal superconscious processes has proven well-nigh impossible — except where the treatment has incorporated an emotional seizure analogous to Mesmer's crisis. Quite possibly, the very fact that superconscious therapy has become respectable has destroyed its effectiveness for such patients, and a mental tumult similar to a spontaneous emotionally-charged religious conversion of the kind actively discouraged by all major religions, will always be needed to break such an emotional disturbance. Electro-shock therapy was invented for just such a purpose, and while EST is now generally condemned in the strongest possible terms, the theory behind it is by no means discredited.

It must be understood that Mesmer was not some obscure country doctor trying to make a fast name for himself. At the time of his first experiments he was one of the most respected physicians in Vienna, held in high favor at the royal court. He had married a widow of considerable means, and enjoyed entertaining members of the artistic community. The Mozarts were fond of him, and he promoted the young Wolfgang's career whenever possible, including a summer staging of the teenage genius's first opera in the garden of the Mesmers' large estate, an event attended by the socially elite of the city.

Franzl was cured. She later married Mesmer's stepson and bore him three children, so Mesmer would certainly have known if her symptoms had ever returned.

Mesmer's first published paper described his treatment of Franzl in great detail. It also listed several other cures achieved by the same method, including cases of a patient with apoplexy and subsequent lameness, and others suffering from epilepsy, hysteria, depression and fever fits. The quality of the witnesses to the veracity of his claims, notably Father Hell, guaranteed him an immediate degree of fame. However, his misinterpretation of his discovery, coupled with the fact that skeptical physicians who attempted to replicate Mesmer's mumbojumbo *without* the accompanying positive suggestions found it to be worthless, also guaranteed him accusations of charlatanism and humbuggery. As early as 1779 Mesmer felt the need to publish his *Memoir on the Discovery of Animal Magnetism*, in which he not only spelled out his theory and chronicled

— 29 —

the cases in which it had been applied, but also attempted to refute the allegations of his critics, some of whom appear not to have acted in good faith.

Among the latter was a Dutch doctor named Ingenhousze. Ingenhousze came to Mesmer an avowed skeptic, and gave every appearance of leaving satisfied and convinced. Since we have only Mesmer's account of this incident, I shall allow him to present his own case:[16]

> I invited Mr. Ingenhousze to call. He came, accompanied by a young physician. The patient was then in a fainting fit with convulsions .... I told him to approach the patient, while I withdrew from her, instructing him to touch her. She made no movement. I recalled him to me, and communicated animal magnetism to him by taking him by the hands; I then bade him approach the patient once more, while I kept at a distance, telling him to touch her a second time. This resulted in convulsive movements .... Always to his great astonishment, he brought about a convulsive effect in the part he touched. When this operation was over, he told me he was convinced ....
> I pointed my finger at the patient at a distance of eight paces; the next instant, her body was in convulsion to the point of raising her on the bed with every appearance of pain. I continued, in the same position, to point my finger at the patient, placing Mr. Ingenhousze between herself and me. She underwent the same sensations. Having repeated these tests to Mr. Ingenhousze's satisfaction, I asked him if he was convinced of the marvelous properties about which I had told him, offering to repeat our proceedings if he were not. His reply was to the effect that he wished for nothing further and was convinced. Two days later I was astonished to hear that Mr. Ingenhousze was making statements in public that were quite the reverse of his utterances in my house, and was denying the success of the different experiments he had witnessed .... He was endeavoring to damage my reputation by spreading the report that with the aid of

a number of magnetized pieces which he had brought with him, he had succeeded in unmasking me, proving that it was nothing but a ridiculous prearranged fraud.

At least Dr. Ingenhousze based his denunciation of Mesmer on an experiment conducted by Mesmer himself, and not, as did later detractors, on the performances of persons claiming to be Mesmer's followers. That Mesmer gave an accurate account of Ingenhousze's actions, as he perceived them, can be inferred from the fact that the incident had occured five years before Mesmer wrote it down. By the time Mesmer wrote about Ingenhousze, he had won such success in Paris that he could have ignored persons claiming to have refuted his theories, as safely as Isaac Newton could have ignored persons claiming to have refuted his theory of gravity.

Ingenhousze appears to have acted in bad faith, either by pretending to be convinced by demonstrations that struck him as collusion, and not giving Mesmer the opportunity to refute those suspicions; or by concluding only afterwards that he had been deceived, and pretending that he had "seen through" Mesmer from the start. But that is by no means the only possible explanation of Ingenhousze's seeming hypocrisy.

What Ingenhousze may have done is point his allegedly magnetized finger at the patient when neither she nor Mesmer knew that he was doing so. Naturally she would not have reacted, and Ingenhousze would have been fully justified in concluding that the patient was reacting, not to any non-existent magnetism, but to Mesmer's instruction that she react. Today we recognize that no superconscious subject can respond to a suggestion that never reaches him. But to Ingenhousze, testing for a fluidic force that, if real, would work even in the absence of the patient's awareness that it had been unleashed, his conclusion that he had unmasked Mesmer as a humbug was reasonable. In the 1920s, a similar tactic unmasked N-rays as the discoverer's delusion.

Mesmer was not a humbug; but nonetheless allegations of humbuggery followed him throughout his life. He knew that his methods worked, but he failed to recognize which part of his methodology it was that worked. That meant that any replication of Mesmer's methods that excluded the suggestion to the patient, "This is going to work," was doomed to failure.

Mesmer was a scientist. He observed that the fluctuations of nervous disorders bore some resemblance to current beliefs about the workings of magnetism, formulated a theory of "animal magnetism," conducted experiments designed to test that theory — and achieved the predicted results. That he fell victim to the "dirty test tube syndrome" — failure to rule out alternative explanations for those results — can be attributed to the prescientific standards of his culture. By the standards of his own day, Mesmer acted impeccably.

Mesmer proved himself a shrewd observer and an insightful theorist on several other occasions. He recognized the homeostasis (normal condition) of the human body, and declared that the removal of an interfering factor would allow the body to return to its normal state in the same way that the removal of an interfering magnet allowed a magnetized needle to return to its original orientation.[17] He recognized that, "There exists in Nature a universally acting principle" capable of healing most ills "with or without the help of Medicine."[18] He theorized that the hypothetical magnetic fluid that permeated his universe manifested itself as gravity.[19] He described heat as, "the internal movement of a subtle material,"[20] at a time when many physicists lacked such insight. He even declared that, "Fluidity and solidity should be considered as a relative state of motion and repose of the particles among themselves."[21]

Mesmer recognized the subjective nature of "oracular statements, inspirations, the sibyls, the prophets, divination, witchcraft, magic, the demonology of the ancients; and, in our day, of convulsion and of being possessed." He declared that, "I am able to prove today, that whatever has been true of such phenomena, we should attribute to the same cause, and they should be considered only as variations of the condition called somnambulism."[22]

Despite his refusal to recognize that his own "magnetism" results were achieved by suggestion, Mesmer did recognize that suggestion could play a role in "magnetic" treatment. He thereby pointed the way for the "hypnotists" who succeeded the "mesmerists": "In regard to the effects of animal magnetism, and particularly of the critical sleep, which is one of the most striking phenomena of its application . . . . The perfection of this critical sleep varies according to . . . a kind of education that we give them in this state, and by the manner in which we direct their facilities." [23]

Mesmer also theorized that, "A sleeping man can have insight into his maladies, and distinguish, from among all substances, those which contribute to his conservation and cure." [24] That was by no means an implausible hypothesis, and only two centuries of unsuccessful experimentation enable us to see that in this case also Mesmer was wrong.

Mesmer openly named "possession" among the effects that he attributed to "somnambulism." While he was in Munich, Mesmer was asked his opinion of Father Gassner, currently performing "miracle" cures and exorcisms throughout Bavaria. Mesmer wrote of the case: [25]

> Between the years 1774 and 1775 an ecclesiastic, a man of good faith but of excessive zeal, was operating in the diocese of Ratisbon on various disorders of a nervous nature, using means that appeared to be supernatural to the less well informed in that district. His reputation extended to Vienna, where society was divided into two halves: one regarded his methods as imposture and fraud, while the other looked upon them as miracles performed by Divine power. Both, however, were wrong, and my experience at once told me that the man in question was nothing but a tool of nature.

In other words, Mesmer concluded two hundred years ago that faithhealers' successes were due to "Nature's universally acting principle," directed by "education that we gave them in this state," or as we would label it today, superconscious suggestion. And Mesmer's opinion of exorcism was clearly endorsed by Pope Pius VI, who ordered that all of Gassner's writings on the reality of possession be placed on the Index of Prohibited Books. [26]

Mesmer was at times an intemperate man, responding to medical committees which examined his magnetism theories and found them wanting, as if they had labelled him a charlatan. Considering that his theories *were* totally wrong, the report of the Berlin Academy of Sciences in 1775, which concluded that Mesmer should be "suspected of making false inferences,"[27] was remarkably restrained. But he was also a man of compassion and integrity. He ignored critics who accused him of unethical behaviour that degraded himself and his profession. The behaviour in question was his treating the rich and the poor alike, and publicly advertising in a Paris journal that he would give consultations free. And as a man of convictions, he rejected an offer of a pension from Queen Marie Antoinette when he recognized it as a bribe to stop claiming that he had discovered a new form of medicine.[28]

Toward the end of his life Mesmer became disillusioned that his theories and methods were not universally accepted, but he was never disgraced, and cannot be considered to have died an outcast. A newspaper in 1787 had no doubt of his warranted fame:[29]

> His name is honored in France, in America, in India, in Constantinople. From all parts he receives letters showing proof of esteem, admiration and gratitude. His teaching and healing art prospers in twenty-two schools . . . .

And on that I rest my case for the legitimate place in history of Franz Anton Mesmer.

CHAPTER THREE
ON MESMER'S COATTAILS

Columbus discovered two new continents on the west side of the Atlantic Ocean. Amerigo Vespucci recognized, as Columbus had not, that they *were* new continents, and consequently Columbus's discoveries are today called *America*, not *Columbia*.

Mesmer discovered the therapeutic uses of superconscious suggestion. Mesmer's successors recognized, as Mesmer had not, that suggestion given to a patient in a sleep-like state of relaxation was the true explanation of Mesmer's successes. Consequently, Mesmer's discovery is today best known as *hypnotism*, not *mesmerism*.

For fifty years after Mesmer's death, however, "hypnotism" and "mesmerism" schools flourished as bitter rivals. Although they both used the same methods, each regarded the other's *explanation* of its successes as nonsense. Hypnotism eventually won out, and today the only persons who refuse to believe that patients healed by suggestion therapy are simply talked into healing themselves, are faithhealers.

Please note that adherents of almost all religions believe that, on rare occasions, a prayer for health may be answered, and I have no quarrel with that belief. But the only religions that do not recognize *most* faithhealing as a form of suggestion therapy, are fringe sects whose beliefs and money-grabbing antics have long been an embarrassment to the more traditional churches.

The theory of animal magnetism is dead, and most of Anton Mesmer's techniques have been abandoned by superconscious practitioners in recognition that suggestion can be administered in more dignified and less outlandish ways. But mesmeric practices *do* survive, not in science but in quasi-religious fringe cults. I refer to the continued use of Mesmer's techniques by cultists who believe that the techniques themselves have a metaphysical efficacy.

For example, in 1775 Mesmer's belief in a magnetic basis for his methods led him to invent a "magnetic chain." He constructed a large wooden tub, large enough to accommodate about thirty people, and garnished it with magnetic and occult trappings. He himself wore an outrageous, theatrical robe and carried an iron wand. His patients were seated inside the tub, the lights were dimmed, incense was burned, heavy drapes surrounded the room to absorb and deaden extraneous noises, and restful music was played. The patients, in order to create the "magnetic chain," were instructed each to hold the hands of the persons on either side.

That was the ritual rejected by Mesmer's own followers as flamboyant, unnecessary, and incompatible with the dignity of a scientist and physician. That identical rigmarole, although with a table replacing the tub, is ritualistically followed by spiritualists to this day.

Spiritualism, once accorded the dignity of a religion but now more commonly regarded as a hoax used to swindle gullible old ladies, reached its peak at the turn of the century. Thanks partly to the exposes of the most famous spirit mediums by investigative magicians such as Houdini, and partly to denunciation by the traditional churches, it is today a very minor sect, flourishing mainly in England.

Mesmer's "magnetic chain" is an extremely valuable tool to the fraudulent "mediums" who prey upon believers. Through its use the medium can create the illusion of being physically restrained, since both of his/her hands are seen to be held by the persons on either side before and after the lights are extinguished. In fact such mediums are skilled at extricating themselves and deluding witnesses into holding each other's hands in the dark, in the belief that they are still holding the medium's hands.

THE SUPERCONSCIOUS WORLD

Mesmer merely dimmed the lights to create an occult atmosphere at his "magnetic" sessions. The spook crooks are obliged to extinguish them altogether, so that the medium is freed to wander unseen around the room. He is thus enabled to create various "spirit" manifestations at a distance, even though he is still thought to be effectively prevented from leaving his seat at the seance table. In view of the impossibility of performing any such deceptions in the light, it is no wonder that the "spirits" are shy and refuse to reveal themselves except in the dark. As for the billet reading that constitutes the highlight of spiritualist "church" services, my youngest son could do similar mental conjuring with far more showmanship at the age of eleven.

There is an old show business story that seems appropriate at this point. A vaudeville ventriloquist, finding himself out of work, utilized his ventriloquial experience to become a spirit medium. He was an instant success, and people came from far and wide to hear the voices of the "dead" coming from beneath the table, above their heads, or from out of a vase. After one such session a dear old widow approached our self-styled medium and pushed a hundred-dollar bill into his hand. "I'll return next week alone," she whispered, "and if you can make my late husband talk to me I'll give you a further two hundred dollars."

"Madam," he replied, "for two hundred dollars, not only will your husband talk to you, but I'll drink a glass of water while he does it."

Mesmer invented the seance, the hand-holding magnetic chain still utilized by spiritualists. So do the spiritualists acknowledge their debt to Mesmer? They do not.

It is a sad fact of history that innovators, revisionists and renegades tend to despise their spiritual ancestors. Founders of new religions usually reserve their strongest vitriole for those whose beliefs they have replaced. When Houdini felt that he had eclipsed Robert-Houdin, whose name he had usurped, he wrote *The Unmasking of Robert Houdin*, in the belief that he could minimize his status as a copyist by denigrating the man he had copied. Hitler denounced Stalin, whose mass murders he then proceeded to duplicate. And Michel Gauquelin denounced the sun-sign astrologers, as if by doing so he could make his new astrology, "astrobiology," any less absurd and falsifiable than theirs.

In view of this, it should come as no surprise that spiritualists denounce both the mental illusionists whose conjuring tricks they copy, and hypnotism, deriving as it does from the mesmeric seance that the spook crooks appropriated for their own nefarious purpose. And if anyone doubts that spiritualism is a form of self-delusion, commonly called self-hypnosis, he has only to look at Sherlock Holmes' creator, Sir Arthur Conan Doyle, who remained an adamant believer in the spirits in the face of both Houdini's exposé of every single medium to whom Doyle introduced him, and the confession by the Fox sisters, the inventors of spiritualism, that they had perpetrated a hoax.

High on the list of organizations and identifiable groups that denounce "malicious animal magnetism, hypnotism and suggestion," but which owe their very existence to Mesmer's discovery, is the sect founded by Mary Baker Eddy a century ago and known today as Christian Science. The President of the British Society of Medical Hypnotists has denounced, "this extraordinary cult which has the impertinence to call itself Christian," as "neither Christian nor Scientific." [1]

For my part, I think that any person who takes it upon himself to decide who is or is not entitled to call himself a Christian, is a fanatic by definition; and Van Pelt is as much a fanatic (and an anti-Semitic one at that[2]) as any of the persons he condemns. It is a great pity that such a well-written, useful and, in the main, factual book as Van Pelt's *Hypnotism and the Power Within* contains so many passages that can only be described as unbridled bigotry, and I strongly suspect that that is the reason it was never published in the USA. I therefore do not dispute that Christian Science is Christian. But if it is a science, then physics and chemistry are not.

Mary Baker Eddy was at best mentally unstable, and after she started claiming to have raised the dead (without the mass media ever managing to locate, let alone interview, one of the former corpses), her son narrowly failed to convince a lunacy court that she should be institutionalized for her own protection.

Mrs. Eddy's career began with her meeting with Phineas Quimby, a mesmerist, in 1862. At the time she was suffering from hysterical paralysis, and had been confined to bed for several years. Her paralysis was apparently

THE SUPERCONSCIOUS WORLD

the culmination of forty years of hysterical fits, neurotic hallucinations and psychosomatic delusions.[3]

Phineas Quimby was a watchmaker who, in 1848, saw a performance by mesmerist Charles Poyen and decided that he could make more money from mesmeric healing than from watchmaking. He acquired a "professional subject," a seventeen-year-old boy named Lucius Burkmar, whom he "mesmerized" in the presence of ailing patients. Burkmar, utilizing the "clairvoyance" that somnambulists were then believed to possess, diagnosed the patients' illnesses and prescribed the drugs that would heal them.

Then one day Burkmar prescribed a drug that Quimby deemed too expensive, so he replaced it with a cheap look-alike — and the resultant placebo effected a complete cure. At that point Quimby independently realised, what the hypnotists had known for half a century but the mesmerists still refused to acknowledge, that the true therapeutic element in his rigmarole was his *suggestion* to the patient that the prescription would cure him. Quimby, who was no charlatan, fired his somnambulistic assistant and set himself up as the world's first talk therapist. A little later, having doubts about the insubstantial nature of suggestion, Quimby formulated the theory of "mind cure" that a Bangor, Maine, newspaper described as follows:[4]

> He says that the mind is what it thinks it is, and that if it contends against the thought of disease and creates for itself an ideal form of health, that form impresses itself upon the animal spirit and through that upon the body.

In that summation by Phineas Quimby of his theory of mind cure, we can see the origin of Christian Science.

Mrs. Eddy (to avoid confusion I use her later name, although she had not yet met Mr. Eddy) consulted Quimby in 1862, and he cured her by the talk therapy that we would now call superconscious suggestion. She became his devoted disciple, and until his death in 1866 actively promoted "P.P. Quimby's Healing of Disease by Spiritual Science." However, even from the beginning of her association with Quimby, Mrs.

Eddy had been harboring revisionist theories of her own concerning the mechanisms behind his methods.

After Quimby's death Mrs. Eddy incorporated into the Christian Science that she established the non-Quimbian amendment that, more than anything else she ever did, reveals just how distorted and dysfunctional her thought processes really were.

The human body, according to Mary Baker Eddy, does not exist! Matter does not exist. The universe does not exist. You do not exist. I do not exist. Since the body does not exist, obviously it can never fall ill. Illness does not exist. Belief in the body is "error." Belief in illness is "error." To this day Christian Scientists refuse to consult doctors — unless of course they become sick.

Russell Braddon tells an interesting anecdote in his autobiographical, *The Naked Island*. During the Second World War, Braddon was interned in a Japanese prison camp near Singapore. He reported that both the Australian and British officers in the camp became alarmed when a sect (guess which?) sprang up among the prisoners, which believed that its members needed no medicines of any kind to combat the malaria and other harsh ills of prison life. The sect attracted fifty members, and the allied officers feared that it would grow larger. But as Braddon wryly commented, after the last of the fifty had died there didn't seem to be any further interest.

The first edition of Mrs. Eddy's *Science and Health* was published in 1875. It was essentially an expanded version of a manuscript by Quimby. It contained so many errors of fact, inconsistencies, and evidences of a mind not in control of itself, that had it not been revised, Mrs. Eddy's weird fantasy would have died with her. But it was rewritten, by competent ghost-writers, as many times as there were new editions. One of Mrs. Eddy's editors, James Henry Wiggin, even added Greek, Latin and Sanskrit etymologies to create the impression that Mrs. Eddy was a scholar.

The most notable changes in succeeding editions of the Eddy Scripture, was the softening of Mrs. Eddy's attacks upon the medical profession. This was hardly surprising, since she eventually felt the need for glasses, false teeth, and painkilling injections for kidney stones. She did not, however, seek medical treatment for all of her ailments, and when her "non-existent" body expired of pneumonia, she suffered the ultimate "error" of believing she was dead!

Mary Baker Eddy was cured of chronic psychosomatic incapacities by suggestion posing as magnetism, and founded a religion in which misunderstood superconscious suggestion is the only permitted form of therapy. It is therefore both understandable and ironic that the sect denounces as satanic the very form of talk therapy on which it is itself based, and which it continues to utilize on its members whether they are suffering from the eighty percent of ailments that will heal themselves with or without treatment of any kind, or the twenty percent that superconscious suggestion cannot, and in their case does not, cure.

It is not my purpose to denounce any religious belief as being less commendable or less valid than any other. However, since Christian Scientists deem themselves free to pin a "satanist" label on the very form of medicine (and in my case entertainment) *practised by their own healers*, a form of medicine accepted as a branch of science by the churches of Rome, Canterbury, and Salt Lake City, I consider myself fully justified in suggesting that they set their own house in order before telling others what they may or may not believe. And lest I be accused of presenting a one-sided viewpoint, let me quote from an author who leaned over backwards to present Mrs. Eddy's creation in the most favorable light:[5]

> Few people would deny that Mrs. Eddy was domineering, quarrelsome, selfish, greedy, and a liar. It is equally undeniable that she founded a religion that brought comfort to millions. She clearly had a message that filled some need.

The only other reasonably large religion that denounces superconscious science as evil, is the Jehovah's Witnesses. Just why Charles Russell's followers have such a belief is uncertain. Biographies of the sect's architects that I have consulted make no mention of the kind of hypnotic or mesmeric connection that can be traced as with Mrs. Eddy. Nor does the sect reject medicine, except in connection with blood transfusions, and use misunderstood superconscious suggestion in its place. And nowhere in even their own Bible translation[6] did I find any passage that, by the wildest misinterpretation, can be construed as a prohibition of suggestion-therapy. I can only conclude, therefore, that the reverend Russell *did* have an unfortunate encounter with a mesmerist, and that it permanently clouded his thinking.

Religion *per se* is not hostile to manipulation of the superconscious. Some minor religious sects are hostile, and so are some individuals within other religions. In many cities I have presented my show in auditoriums owned by the Catholic Church, and the parish priest has helped promote ticket sales. But individual priests, like individual doctors and individual bartenders, can have their own beliefs and predilections.

I fondly remember one amusing incident in my career when I wished to play a couple of nights in the parish hall of a small town called Bega, in New South Wales, Australia. The local priest was a nice old man of Irish descent, and when I told him that it would be an evening of hypnotism (a word and technique I was still using at the time), he looked very worried and said, "I'm afraid the Bishop might object to my renting the hall for that." So I told him I was thinking of giving twenty-five percent to the church, rather than paying a fixed rent. "Well then, I don't know that you're a hypnotist, do I now?" was his instant reply.

There have been cities in which I performed where the local priest has labelled as "black magic" the same show that played a Catholic hall fifty miles away, and ordered his parishioners not to attend. A religion cannot be held accountable for the personal opinions of all of its members. Human nature being what it is, persons who are stubbornly superstitious, simple-minded or intolerant can become priests, ministers or rabbis as easily as they can become politicians, lawyers or even doctors.

And speaking of doctors: There is one other group that many people imagine to be universally opposed to the demonstration of superconscious science on stage. That is the medical hypnotists. Individuals within that group who make public statements concerning stage performances, have a pronounced tendency to pretend that they speak for their profession. They most certainly do not.

I have worked with medical hypnotists at the University of Utah and elsewhere, and shown some of them how to improve their techniques.

And I am acquainted with many others who came to my show with some reservations and went away totally satisfied with the positive image of superconscious suggestion that I convey to my audiences. I do not pretend that *they* speak for their profession — but neither do the detractors.

There are many individual medical hypnotists who form beliefs based on inadequate evidence, beliefs they prove quite incapable of modifying in the light of later observations. They consequently seek every opportunity to condemn practitioners outside of their profession in order to promote their own interests. High on the list of such hypocritical loudmouths is the aforementioned Dr. Van Pelt of the British Medical Hypnotists' Association. Such individuals hint at dark troubles for those who are hypnotized by anyone other than a medical doctor. But they themselves, with rare exceptions, have no more knowledge of superconscious suggestion than they have been able to acquire in a handful of weekend seminars and workshops. Yet they cry wolf without one scrap of evidence to back their assertions up. If hypnotism is so inherently dangerous, just what is there about a medical degree that causes that danger to vanish? And why do they then dabble in a form of treatment that they themselves categorize as dangerous?

Actually, I am not unsympathetic to some of the arguments put forward by some of the medical hypnotists who oppose stage demonstrations, and I have made a point from the day I first stepped on stage to present an entertainment that would enlighten my audience as well as entertain it.

For example, many of the would-be entertainers who rent the cheapest hall in town or play the lowest bars, and proceed to demonstrate everything they have learned about hypnotism from a "You too can be the life of the party" manual, do indeed give the public an impression of the superconscious state that is every bit as false and ridiculous as the nonsense peddled by the worst kind of television script writers. I have always made sure that my audience understands the following basic principles:

- No superconscious subject can be compelled to commit any action that violates his personal moral code.
- No superconscious subject can fail to awaken.
- While a major portion of the population can achieve

a degree of superconsciousness, only about one in twenty can achieve the depth necessary to react to hallucinations.
- Superconscious suggestion can cure non-functional nervous disorders and modify nervous habits, but it cannot cure broken bones, alcohol-damaged livers, or diseases caused by bacteria or viruses. It is not a panacea, and while it has great value as a supportive therapy, it will never replace traditional medicine.
- Some so-called hypnotists have in fact used stooges, and audiences have seen subjects give rehearsed responses to inadequate suggestions. In North America this practice is more common than not. I never use stooges, and consider myself adequately skilled at detecting simulators who pretend to me and the audience that they are superconscious when they are not. Consequently, if a simulator who had hitherto escaped detection were to do or say anything that a genuinely superconscious subject could not do or say, the audience would see me ask him to leave the stage and realize why. As a general rule I try not to embarrass such persons, since their action is usually not malicious and the embarrassment of getting caught is quite sufficient without holding the individual up to public ridicule.

All valid criticism of stage demonstrations is satisfied and answered by the above, and those medical hypnotists who have seen my show have usually complimented me for giving an accurate, informative demonstration of a scientific discipline. A small number have, however, remained hostile, and on being asked to state a specific objection to anything I did, they gave me the impression of suffering from the most lamentable of old-fashioned human weaknesses: pure jealousy. It seems that some doctors desire a form of trade union exclusivity.

Considerably more medical hypnotists have applauded my show than attacked it. After I had performed at Salt Lake City, Utah, in 1973, I was recruited by a group of medical doctors in that city to work with them to discover new uses for my techniques in the medical field, as well as give a series of lectures to the medical and psychiatry departments at the

University of Utah. It was those same doctors who signed the necessary sponsorship guarantees to obtain for me the status of a permanent resident of the United States. I remained in Utah for a year in fulfillment of my commitment, and only my love for the theater impelled me to return to the stage.

There is one other group that, like the Christian Scientists, owes its origin to the theories of Anton Mesmer, and which continues to use mesmeric mumbojumbo in its rituals. Also like the Christian Scientists, it stubbornly refuses to recognize that any successes it ever achieves (and they are rare) are due solely to superconscious suggestion. That group is the psychoanalysts.

Psychoanalysts do not condemn hypnotism as diabolic. Rather, they prefer to damn it with faint praise, declaring that, "It may occasionally be useful, but the results are not permanent."[7] In fact psychoanalysis came into existence because its inventor, Sigmund Freud, was a fifth-rate hypnotist and as such needed an alternative method of curing psycho-neurotic patients, some of whose mental illnesses were almost as severe as Freud's own. Freud would today be considered at best as a borderline psychotic who should be institutionalized before treatment could begin; at least that would be the diagnosis of any person adhering rigidly to the guidelines established by his present-day devotees.

According to the most exhaustive study of Freud and his theories and practices so far published, M.L. Gross's *The Psychological Society*:[8]

> Sigmund Freud suffered from a spastic colon, near-continuous depressive moods, neurasthenia, homosexual tendencies, bad temper, migraines, constipation, travel phobias, infected sinuses, fainting spells, and hostile drives of hate and murder....
> Freud [was] a victim of superstition, magical numbers, and childish gullibility....
> He was so consumed by the idea of unconscious hate that ... it became to him synonymous with love....
> Freud's self-analysis kept dredging up ... so much anal material that Freud coined a word for it: "Drekkology," a play on the German-Yiddish word for feces....

THE SUPERCONSCIOUS WORLD

Cocaine at first and cigars throughout most of his life were his emotional crutches . . . .
Superstition, mysticism, and an inexplicable naivete, were only pieces of his convoluted neurotic personality . . . .
At the age of seven he walked into his parents' bedroom and intentionally urinated on the floor. He described himself as a victim of *neurasthenia*, a phrase that incorporated modern neuroticism and a form of hypochondriasis . . . .
On his father's side, Freud inherited what he called a possible "neuropathological taint" . . . . The only evidence of "taint" in his immediate family, Freud believed, was his own and his sister Rosa's "pronounced tendencies toward neurasthenia." This tendency showed itself in lifelong indigestion, often with constipation, in an irritable spastic colon, a train phobia and a severe moodiness which tended more toward depression than elation . . . .
Freud once touchingly wrote Fliess: "As you well know, in my life a woman has never been a substitute for a comrade, or friend" . . . . Freud obviously experienced Oedipal lust, a disturbance which non-Freudians, such as child psychiatrist Dr. Stella Chess of New York University, believe affects only a small number of children . . . .
One unusual neurotic symptom was his tendency to faint. He was known to have fainted at least four or five times. Once it was over the sight of hemorrhaging blood. Usually it was because of some slight to his extravagant ego . . . .

In other words, Sigmund Freud was not the ideal man to be treating your loved ones.

I see no need to enlarge on Gross's conclusions. Anyone who doubts their validity can read Gross's book, which is thoroughly researched and impeccably documented.

Sigmund Freud was a Viennese physician. He learned from a friend and colleague, Dr. Breuer, of a cure of a hysterical patient brought about by hypnosis. Freud became interested in the new theory, and studied it under Charcot, Bernheim, and Liebeault, three persons whose roles in the evolution of hypnotism will be mentioned in the next chapter. Unfortunately, he lacked the charisma needed to inspire belief in his abilities, and belief is more important in the practice of suggestion than in any other field. Also, Freud seems never to have learned or realized that the deep state of superconsciousness that only a minority of people can achieve, regardless of the skill of the operator, is quite unnecessary for a medical practitioner's purpose.

Freud did recognize his limitations as a hypnotist. He realized that he would have to find a methodology that, at least for him, would be quicker. He therefore invented a form of treatment that he believed would cure a patient in about five or ten years!

In fact Freud was being overoptimistic. While it is true that most psychoanalysts treat most patients for less than five years, it is invariably the patient who terminates the "therapy" when he realizes that the only thing being cured is his large bank account. The continuing failure of analysts to show that Freud's theories have ever cured anybody of anything, any time, anywhere, would have caused those theories to be abandoned from the outset by any other medical discipline, indeed any scientific discipline. There is a joke in orthodox medical circles that, every time a psychoanalyst cures a patient, he is obliged to throw a "psychovation" and invite every other psychoanalyst on earth to attend (somewhat like a golfer being obliged to buy drinks all round after a hole-in-one.) According to the tale, the first psychovation was held in Vienna in 1879, the second in Paris in 1926, and the third and most recent in Philadelphia in 1953 — but of course I don't believe *that*. At least, I don't think I believe it.

As weird as most of Freud's theories were, they did tend to be conclusions drawn from valid observations. For example, it had long been recognized that traumatic events in the half-forgotten past could cause neurotic behaviour in the present. Evidence of this can be seen in the enormous number of war veterans who have suffered delayed shock syndrome. Freud theorized that *all* psycho-neurotic behaviour could be attributed to shock trauma that dated, not merely from the patient's past, but from his infancy.

THE SUPERCONSCIOUS WORLD

Specifically, Freud concluded early in his career that all hysteria patients had been seduced by adults during childhood. Claustrophobes, he theorized, had not only been locked in cupboards as infants, but had equated the experience with a return to the mother's womb, and had consequently developed guilt feelings as a result of their vicarious consummation of Oedipal incest wishes!

Freud's preoccupation with sex, particularly child-sex, is well known. Admittedly his timing was bad. He published theories of infantile sexuality at a time when Queen Victoria was refusing gifts of silk stockings on the ground that, "The Queen of England has no legs." The Victorians barely acknowledged, in public, that sex existed. Consequently the reaction to Freud's portrayal of six-year-olds as lustful savages who wished to kill the same-sex parent and copulate with the opposite-sex parent was met, not with the indulgent laughter it would have triggered today, but with outrage that had nothing to do with scientific, informed rejection of Freud's nonsense.

While studying hypnosis under Bernheim, Freud noticed that Bernheim had been able to break down his patients' post-hypnotic amnesia by persistent questioning. If events that occurred during hypnosis and were forgotten on awakening could be recalled to memory by questioning, Freud reasoned, then the (non-existent?) traumatic childhood event responsible for adult neuroses could surely be recalled by the same means. Freud concluded that he could dispense with hypnosis altogether, and simply question his patient for as long as it took to make the patient recall the event whose suppression was the cause of his mental imbalance. It might take a few years, but since the therapist would be paid by the hour, so much the better. Only the rich could afford such analysis, but everyone knew that the poor were kept much too busy doing manual labor to have time to develop neuroses.

Most of Freud's theories were developed by attributing to the population at large those motivations, inconsistencies, and inadequacies that he detected in patients who had come to him precisely because they were neurotic. Other generalizations about the masses derived from his projecting on to the mentally healthy the evidence of serious mental disturbance that he saw in the mirror. Freud decreed, in effect, "Since I am normal and you are normal, and I am a sex-obsessed neurotic motivated

THE SUPERCONSCIOUS WORLD

from childhood by lust and hatred, therefore you and the rest of the world are sex-obsessed neurotics motivated from childhood by lust and hatred." Can we really wonder that the analysts who spend months and years searching a patient's memories for evidence of such motivations, very seldom find them? They could with as much hope of success search for Santa Claus and the tooth fairy.

Freud's original technique was to question his patients. But even that he eventually saw as too much like hard work. He evolved instead the practice of simply listening and saying nothing, while the patient spent as many years as his pocket book would allow, saying anything that came into his head. That technique continues to be used by psychoanalysts to this day. It is also used by two other identifiable groups, but with rather more success: prostitutes and bartenders.

As in any dogma, psychoanalysis has its revisionists. Some therapists actually make statements in their patients' presence that are not mere repetitions of the patients' own words: "I feel depressed." "You feel depressed?" "I wonder why I bother coming here." "You wonder why you bother coming here?" Such revisionists, in the process of making original remarks, sometimes accidentally give the patient a clue on how to cure himself. The superconscious element of the patient's laid-back, receptive condition responds to the suggestion and, to the therapist's amazement, effects a cure. Obviously this can happen only when the patient's problem is one that could have been cured by acknowledged superconscious suggestion weeks, months, or even years earlier.

Consider the following case, reported by Van Pelt. The patient consulted a psychiatrist at the age of seventeen, in the hope of being cured of a masturbation habit that he had been culturally conditioned to regard as a perversion. The analyst blandly informed the patient that masturbation was not a perversion, and recommended that he continue the practice throughout the course of psychoanalysis that continued for seven years. What the unenlightened psychiatrist failed to recognize or care about, was that the patient at no time came to *believe* that masturbation was not a perversion. By the age of twenty-four his feelings of guilt had made him a dysfunctional neurotic. The analyst declared him incurable, and he went to a hypnotist — Van Pelt.

THE SUPERCONSCIOUS WORLD

Van Pelt cured him in a matter of days, using the method that psychoanalysts officially reject but which is in fact responsible for all cures that the Freudian devotees have ever achieved: superconscious suggestion. And since Van Pelt recognized that deeply-held beliefs cannot be changed by suggestion, he quite correctly enhanced the patient's ability to make his behaviour conform to his beliefs.

Psychoanalysis is not dead. It is not as fashionable as it was twenty years ago, but it still exists and is dying far too slowly. It has about as much scientific merit as astrology.

Of equal merit with psychoanalysis are those other forms of pseudomedicine that, while not mesmeric in origin, do use superconscious suggestion to cure patients while stubbornly maintaining that the cures are achieved by ritualistic mumbojumbo as intrinsically useless as Mesmer's magnets. These include:

- acupuncture, which has been found to work only on patients conditioned to believe in its validity, or in other words only when used in conjunction with superconscious suggestion.[9]
- osteopathy, which pretends to cure everything from hemophilia to cancer by readjusting mislocated subluxations of the vertebrae. According to medical doctors and anatomists, backed up by X-rays and microphotography, the osteopaths' mystical "subluxations" simply do not exist.
- naturopathy, in which a patient is treated with substances medical doctors have found to have no curative powers whatsoever, diluted to the approximate proportions of one drop of allegedly curative substance dissolved in one Pacific Ocean of distilled water.
- homeopathy, which is also based on substances with no curative powers that medical doctors have ever been able to detect.[10]
- scientology, formerly dianetics, a pseudo-medicine that evolved into a pseudo-religion when founder Ron

THE SUPERCONSCIOUS WORLD

Hubbard realized that quackery does not enjoy the same tax exemption as religion.

Christian Scientists, psychoanalysts, homeopaths, naturopaths, osteopaths, scientologists, acupuncturists and professional faith-healers all practice "mesmerism," superconscious suggestion accompanied by intrinsically valueless ritual that its practitioners delude themselves is the curative factor. It is that superconscious suggestion that is the only element of their disciplines that has ever cured anybody of anything. (Note that "psychic surgeons" are not suggestion therapists, but outright humbugs who use sleight of hand to pass off chicken giblets as magically-excised human tissue, while creating the illusion of plunging their hands deep inside the patient's body.)

CHAPTER FOUR

SUPERCONSCIOUS HISTORY AFTER MESMER

Anton Mesmer lived and died a "mesmerist." That may sound like a tautology — an unnecessary repetition — but it is not. "Mesmerism" denoted a particular theory, and Mesmer never abandoned that theory.

Practically from the start, Mesmer incorporated into his therapy sessions flamboyant theatrical techniques calculated to generate an atmosphere of awe and utilize the full potential of his patients' imaginations. He could not have been unaware that he was doing so. He could not have imagined, for example, that magnetism was "shy," and only willing to manifest itself in a darkened, sound-proofed room in which music was playing. Modern parapsychologists claim that ESP (extra-sensory perception) is "shy" and will not manifest itself in the presence of a magician or skeptical investigator. But they are self-deluded, or in some cases self-serving, whereas Mesmer was merely uninformed. Yet despite his sub-threshold awareness of the role suggestion played in the induction of "magnetism," he died still believing in the reality of an all-permeating subetheric fluid that, had it existed, could just as validly be called "magnetism" as any other name.

Yet also practically from the start, other investigators recognized that the "magnetism" only seemed to work when the patient knew it was being applied. Not having Mesmer's vested interest in maintaining a theory that he had tested and "proven," they began to wonder if the alleged fluidic force that effected so many cures perhaps existed only in the patient's own mind. Could it be that the patient was in fact being *talked into* utilizing some hitherto unknown capacity of the mind to cure himself?

It was one of Mesmer's own students, the Marquis de Puysegur, who first recognized that the superconscious state, which he thought was induced by magnetism and which he labelled "artificial somnambulism" in the belief that it was identical with sleepwalking, was a condition of heightened suggestibility in which a patient could be instructed to cure himself. He made that discovery in 1784 while magnetizing a patient named Victor.

Victor, a twenty-three-year-old peasant, had been in bed with bronchitis for four days when Puysegur got him up and magnetized him. As Puysegur described the incident to a friend:[1]

> What was my surprise, after seven or eight minutes, to see the man go to sleep quietly in my arms, without any convulsion or pain. I accelerated the crisis and brought on delirium; he talked and discussed his business aloud. When it seemed to me that his thoughts were affecting him for the worse, I tried to divert him to lighten his themes; the attempt cost me no great trouble: I soon saw him quite happy in the belief that he was shooting for a prize, dancing at a fete and so on.

Puysegur had discovered, not only that a superconscious subject could be made to believe that his nervous illnesses were being cured, but also that he could be made to accept the reality of hallucinations suggested by the physician. In so doing, he paved the way for demonstrations by entertainers whose performances had nothing to do with the new discovery's therapeutic uses. No doubt there will always be persons who see the transfer of superconscious practice from the surgery to the theater stage as demeaning. But such persons should be aware that singing, dancing and acting came into existence as means of communicating with and worshipping the gods. Aeschylus, Sophocles, and Euripides wrote their great works as acts of homage to Dionysos. Should we then believe that Shakespeare, Caruso, Pavlova, and the Barrymores disgraced art forms that ought to be restricted to their original "higher" purpose?

Puysegur made even more significant discoveries about the somnambulistic "trance." Victor once, while "magnetized," gave Puysegur a valuable document for safekeeping. On awakening he became most distressed when he sought the document in its customary depository and found it to be missing. While awake he had no recollection of anything that had taken place during his somnambulism.[2]

> "The line of demarcation," said Puysegur, " is so complete that these two states may also be described as two separate existences. I have noticed that in the magnetic state, the patients have a clear recollection of all their doings in the normal state; but in the normal state they can recall nothing of what has taken place in the magnetic condition."

It did not occur to Puysegur to compare this post-superconscious amnesia with dreaming, even though the analogy of a sleeper forgetting the content of a dream on awakening was an obvious one. Apparently the watchdog not only protects the individual from harmful external manipulation; it also protects the memory from becoming cluttered to the point of dysfunction, by identifying trivia and removing it from conscious awareness. Since dreams and superconscious fantasies are similarly unreal, both count as trivia. However, just as an association of ideas can cause a dream to be recalled, so some subjects will, after the fact, recall fantasies experienced on stage.

I have long been puzzled as to why so many doctors seem to derive satisfaction from their patients' inability to recall the events that transpired during a therapeutic session, and why they actively promote such amnesia by suggesting that it will occur. This strikes me as questionable medicine. Surely it is better for the patient to be able to recall his experiences, and thereby to recognize that he played a co-operative role in his own cure. My own observations tell me that this is so. And it is on that same point that I also depart from most performers of the suggestive arts on stage. I point out to my volunteers that the events on stage have been part of a created fantasy, and that the talents brought forward at my suggestion are in fact their own. I further inform them that if they feel any need to recall the events of that fantasy, they will be able to do so with clarity and in detail. It seems to me that, if a person on stage shows talents that had not been known to him before, the least I can do is to make sure that he recognizes such talents as purely his own, and not the artificial creation of some benevolent Svengali.

Something else that Puysegur first noticed could never have been predicted. Although his patient, Victor, was normally tongue-tied, inarticulate, outwardly dull-witted, and possessed of the limited vocabulary that was expected of a peasant, when superconscious he became both lucid and intelligent. Today we recognize that even the most culturally deprived person has usually had sufficient exposure to educated vocabulary and thinking patterns, for those patterns to have been impressed into the mind and to be recoverable under superconsciousness.

Puysegur, however, had no such awareness and, in a society that regarded all of the attributes of peasant status as divinely ordained, he can hardly be blamed for seeking explanations of a paranormal or metaphysical nature. In fact he imagined that a somnambulistic subject acquired powers of telepathy and clairvoyance, and that Victor's lucidity was caused by his ability to utilize information received by extra-sensory means from those around him.

Puysegur's observation of a superconscious subject's enhanced intellectual capacities led to two kinds of speculation and experimentation. First of all it appeared to support Mesmer's idea that a patient's mystical insight into his own problem could enable him to diagnose himself and prescribe an effective cure. And secondly it led to the belief that a superconscious subject could clairvoyantly reach into the mind of another person and similarly diagnose and prescribe.

The first person to achieve notoriety as a practitioner of somnambulistic clairvoyant diagnosis was Edgar Cayce. Cayce was not a conscious humbug for, like Mesmer, his belief in his imagined power was quite sincere, and he did cure those patients who would have recovered with no treatment whatsoever, as well as those who could have been cured by any other practitioner of superconscious suggestion.

Even more successful than Cayce was the aforementioned Phineas Quimby. But Quimby came to realize that suggestion alone, and not clairvoyant diagnosis, was responsible for his cures. Cayce did not. For that reason, books on psychic healing by and about Edgar Cayce continue to be peddled to the gullible as fast as hack sensationalists can write and publish them, while Quimby's name is remembered only by historical scholars.

While Puysegur's greatest achievement was undoubtedly the discovery of the superconscious state, a related observation was almost as important. Puysegur cured his first patient by following Mesmer's prescription of inducing a "crisis." But Puysegur came to realize that, since it was suggestion that effected the cure, the dubious and potentially dangerous crisis could be eliminated. Cure by crisis was replaced by cure by somnambulism. And since the hand-holding seance was also recognized by Puysegur as mere flamboyance, an undignified and unnecessary means of stimulating the subject's imagination, that too was eliminated from scientific mesmerism — only to be picked up by the spiritualists, as aforementioned.

The first true hypnotist, the man who recognized that Puysegurian somnambulism not only induced a state of suggestibility in the patient, but was itself induced by auto-concentration, was Abbe Faria, a Portugese priest working in Paris. Faria's most important work, *On the Cause of Lucid Sleep*, was published in 1819, and it spelled out discoveries he had in fact made five years earlier.

Faria replaced the phrase "animal magnetism" with the more accurate term, "concentration." He described how he mesmerized patients by having them concentrate on the idea of going to sleep. And he described the resultant state of superconsciousness, equivalent to Puysegur's somnambulism, as "lucid sleep."

Faria utilized no mystical trappings. Instead he caused the subject to sit down in a comfortable position. He then instructed him to lean back, relax, and concentrate on sleep. His induction of lucid sleep concluded with the command, "Sleep! Sleep!"

Faria's book described not only his treatment of nervous disorders, but also experiments conducted for the pursuit of knowledge. He gave details of how he had induced hallucinations and even caused paralysis and blindness, for the purpose of showing that some instances of those afflictions can be caused by the imagination and therefore cured through the imagination. He reported also giving suggestions to patients in lucid sleep that were obeyed after awakening. This latter phenomenon I term delayed superconscious reaction; but from the time of Braid it has been commonly called post-hypnotic suggestion. Faria made no attempt to explain delayed superconscious reaction, and the first person to do so was unfortunately not a hypnotist but a mesmerist. Consequently his explanation was an elaboration of Mesmer's erroneous magnetism theory.

Faria reached both some insightful and some wrong conclusions. Although he developed some effective techniques for inducing superconsciousness in difficult subjects, he failed to recognize that a degree of suggestibility may have been achieved even though the subject was not sufficiently influenced to accept hallucinations. He thus saw patients who were in fact susceptible enough for most therapeutic applications of suggestion as failures. He therefore concluded that only a minority can be induced into lucid sleep, and attributed the non-reaction of the majority to their obstinate refusal to co-operate. His conclusion was right that people who cannot be induced into any degree of superconsciousness are, consciously or unconsciously, unwilling rather than unable. But he was wrong in concluding that such persons constitute a majority.

In fact it is true that only about five percent of the population can be rendered sufficiently superconscious to accept hallucinations — and only persons who achieve that depth are suitable for the creative demands of my concerts. It is also true that only about ten percent of westerners can be superconsciously anesthetized for the performance of major operations, although the figure is somewhat higher in eastern cultures with a stronger mystical tradition. However, fully ninety-five percent of all people can achieve the depth of relaxed suggestibility to be cured of such nervous habits as smoking or overeating by the direct or recorded voice of a skilled practitioner.

Faria's book did not, as it should have done, wipe out mesmerism and replace it with hypnotism. Not until more than fifty years later, by which time the triumph of suggestion-theory over magnetism-theory was all but total, was Faria's primacy finally recognized. Instead, his findings fell on deaf ears, and it seems likely that hypnotism's co-discoverer, Alexandre Bertrand, was not aware of the existence of Faria's book.

Faria did, however, achieve a dubious distinction by being immortalized in Dumas's *The Count of Monte Cristo*. Because Dumas saw Faria as a man who recognized the error of one theory only to replace it with an alternative that was, Dumas believed, equally erroneous, he incorporated into his book an *Abbe Faria* who spent years tunneling out of a prison cell, one inch at a time, only to wind up, not in the open air but in another cell.

Alexandre Bertrand was the man whose recognition of the suggestion-explanation of mesmerism truly led the way for Braid, Liebeault, and Bernheim. Bertrand's *Treatise on Somnambulism* was published in Paris in 1823, four years after Faria's book; but it showed far greater insight into the true nature of somnambulism or lucid sleep than had Faria, and Bertrand deserves at least equal billing with Faria as the discoverer of scientific hypnotism.

Bertrand first met Mesmer in 1778 when Mesmer invited members of the Paris faculty of medicine to attend his clinic in that city and examine his methods. Bertrand was one of three physicians who accepted the invitation. For two months Mesmer showed them patients who came to him blind and left sighted, came deaf and left able to hear, came lame and left able to walk, and came neurotic and left rational. Bertrand and his colleagues were not impressed. They were, after all, investigating Mesmer's claim to be utilizing an unknown magnetic "fluid" possessed of intrinsically curative properties. They correctly recognized that some healings were only partially successful, some could have been feigned, and those whose authenticity could not be doubted could be explained by the spontaneous healing powers of nature. They reported back to the faculty that, "The facts are undoubtedly amazing, but they are inconclusive."[3]

Bertrand did not, however, forget what he had seen. He remained convinced that Mesmer's "animal magnetism" was explainable by other means but, satisfied that Mesmer had discovered *something*, he began to conduct his own investigations. By 1820 he was himself lecturing on somnambulism phenomena, and three years later published his interpretation.

Bertrand rejected Mesmer's fluidist theory of a physical force that passed from mesmerizer to subject, and co-authored the animist theory that the force was not physical but psychological. For convenience I have been using the words mesmerists and hypnotists to describe proponents of the conflicting theories of superconsciousness (and will continue to do so); but strictly speaking there were no hypnotists before Braid, and the two schools were more accurately fluidists and animists.

Puysegur had discovered that somnambulistic patients could be made to believe fantasies and to perform physical acts consistent with the fantasies. For example, Puysegur had suggested to Victor that he was at a fete, and Victor had obediently danced. On awakening, Victor had been unaware that he had done so.

Bertrand did not specifically postulate that there were limits to the kind of fantasy a superconscious subject could be made to accept; but he made the discovery from which such limits could have been inferred. He wrote that, "If, for any reason whatsoever, somnambulists have the will to remember anything, they never fail to remember it."[4]

If it were possible, by creating an appropriate alternative reality, for a hypnotist to have a subject commit a crime or non-consensual intimacy, it would be absolutely essential for the hypnotist's purpose that the subject not remember doing so. In discovering that a subject could not be made to forget anything he chose to remember, Bertrand in effect discovered that the penny-dreadful concept of an unscrupulous hypnotist misusing his helpless subject was completely impossible — long before the creator of Svengali and other writers suggested that it *was* possible. And one hundred and sixty years after Bertrand's discovery, the delusion that Bertrand effectively debunked continues to be propagated by the ignorant pens of scriptwriters whose creative energies, I strongly suspect, come more from the consumption of artificial stimulants than from any gray matter they have left in their addled brains. Or perhaps they are pure prostitutes, peddling what they know to be superstition because, "That's what sells, man."

At the same time that Faria, Bertrand, and others were taking Mesmer's discovery toward the animist direction that would result in a true understanding of its nature, the fluidists were not sitting idly by and allowing themselves to be superseded without a fight. They vigorously rejected the animists' explanation of mesmeric phenomena as suggestion.

However, while they were not willing to test the animists' claim that Mesmer was basically wrong, neither were they guilty of total dogmatic adhesion to all of their founder's teachings.

In 1813, while Mesmer was still alive, J.P. Deleuze published, in Paris, his *Critical History of Animal Magnetism*, in which he declared the magnetic fluid to be, not universal as Mesmer imagined, but personal. Deleuze wrote that, "Most somnambulists see a luminous and brilliant fluid enveloping the magnetizer and flowing with greatest force from his head and his hands."[5]

That a luminous fluid, or *aura* as the occultists who borrowed Deleuze's concept later called it, was seen by a majority of the patients of a practitioner who believed in its reality, is not surprising. Once an individual is led to believe that a particular event will occur, whether it be a visual or auditory hallucination or a physical reaction, the onset of even the lightest state of superconsciousness will cause the event to happen. Deleuze's subjects were led to expect that they would see his aura, and therefore they saw it. Bertrand's subjects, being led to expect nothing of the sort, saw nothing.

Because Deleuze believed in his personal fluidic aura, and his belief was reinforced every time one of his patients dutifully "saw" it, he incorporated the aura into the first considered, albeit erroneous, explanation of delayed superconscious reaction. According to Deleuze, the fluid entered the patient's nervous system during the mesmeric trance, took impressions and stored them. Consequently, any "post-hypnotic suggestion" was recorded and imprinted in the patient's physiology, programming the appropriate organs to respond in a suggested manner at a designated signal. That there might be limits to the kind of post-hypnotic suggestion a subject would obey, did not occur to Deleuze or any other fluidist, for the obvious reason that if the magnetic-fluid theory had been correct, there would not have been any limits.

Deleuze's personal-fluid theory led to Elliotson and Esdaile and on to ultimate oblivion. Bertrand's animist theory led to Braid and hypnotism. Perhaps I should state at this point that my own theory of the superconscious does not supersede Braid the way Braid superseded Mesmer. Rather, I abandoned the word hypnotism because it has acquired misleading connotations that Braid would have been the first to repudiate.

In 1837 a Parisian mesmerist, Baron Dupotet, took his fluidist interpretation to London, where he created quite a furor with demonstrations of induced somnambulism. Among those who witnessed and were favorably impressed by Dupotet's demonstrations, was Dr. John Elliotson of the London University Hospital. Elliotson had first displayed some interest in mesmerism after seeing it demonstrated by Richard Chenevix, a pupil of Abbe Faria, in 1829; but only after encountering Dupotet did he commence his own investigations.

Elliotson was open-minded to a fault. On the one hand, he was sufficiently receptive to new discoveries to be the first physician in England to obtain and use a stethoscope. He attacked as ridiculous the common practice of prescribing marriage for hysterical women, the rationale for such prescription being that such women's real problem was night starvation. Elliotson pointed out that hysteria, despite its name, had no connection with the *hystera*, uterus, and in fact was "not confined to the female sex, but occured in boys and men. Mesmerism, not marriage, was the appropriate treatment for hysteria." [6] He recognized that medicine followed indefensible fashions. For thirty years, he said, the liver had been blamed for all ailments that in fact physicians were unable to diagnose correctly. Currently the kidneys had become fashionable. He declared that bloodletting, far from curing any ill, had caused thousands of deaths. He foreshadowed child-protection laws by railing against parental cruelty. And he advocated, in a country that to this day has refused to adopt such a measure, the separation of church and state that had already at the time been part of the American Constitution for more than fifty years: [7]

> Dissenters are to be compelled to pay toward the support of schools where religions are taught of which they disapprove, and the schools are to be under the absolute control of the clergy . . . . There ought to be a national system of education apart from religious belief and sectarian influence.

On the other hand, while Elliotson was able to recognize spiritualism as a sham, he eagerly embraced the equally erroneous doctrines of clairvoyance, phrenology, odylic force, metal-therapy and psychic prophecy.

Since his claims on behalf of mesmerism invariably incorporated the common fluidist belief that mesmerism enhanced the magnetic fluid's capacity to convey information from the past to the future, we should not be surprised that his more rational position on therapeutic mesmerism was treated as the ramblings of a fanatic. We see sadly similar situations today in persons who win recognition in one field, only to destroy their credibility by pontificating in other fields in which they have no comparable competence.

Elliotson advocated much nonsense, and as a fluidist he retained the mesmeric seance long abandoned by the animists. He was therefore subjected to much well-deserved criticism. But he was also subjected to much undeserved criticism, some merely anti-everything-new, but some patently ridiculous. To Elliotson, mesmerism's greatest value was its ability to induce total anesthesia so that major operations could be performed without the patient feeling any pain. When Elliotson read to the Royal Medical and Chirurgical Society a paper on a thigh amputation performed on a mesmerized patient, one doctor declared that the patient was an imposter who merely pretended to feel no pain.

Another proposed that all record of Elliotson's paper should be deleted from the Society's minutes. He asserted that:[8]

> If the history of the man experiencing no agony during the operation were true, the fact was unworthy of their consideration because the pain was a wise provision of nature, and patients ought to suffer pain while their surgeons were operating; they were all the better for it and recovered better.

Elliotson's practice of mesmerism on his patients brought the University Hospital into disrepute and angered his superiors. The situation was not helped by Elliotson's making no move to curb those subjects who, picking up their physician's belief that such things were possible, proclaimed that "magnetic sleep" gave them prophetic powers. One, Elizabeth Okey, formed the habit of wandering into the men's ward at twilight and prophesying who was to die — within the allegedly dying patient's hearing. Even then, it was recognized by many that Elizabeth's behaviour may well have hastened some patients' deaths.

THE SUPERCONSCIOUS WORLD

Recommendations to Elliotson from the dean of the university and others that he abandon his experiments were ignored. In retaliation the university council passed a resolution in 1838, "That the Hospital Committee be instructed to take such steps as they shall deem most advisable to prevent the practice of mesmerism within the hospital."[9] Elliotson immediately resigned his professorship.

In 1843 Elliotson published *Numerous Cases of Surgical Operations Without Pain in the Mesmeric State*, in London. That same year he founded a mesmerism journal, *Zoist*, that appeared quarterly until 1885 and ran articles on mesmeric successes, including more painless operations, that the orthodox medical journals refused to carry. Elliotson himself was a frequent contributor. So was a physician currently practising in India, Dr. James Esdaile.

Esdaile's first acquaintance with mesmerism came from the writings of Elliotson. On April 4, 1845, when Esdaile was in charge of a native hospital in the town of Hoogly, a Hindu convict was scheduled to undergo a painful operation. Esdaile decided to try mesmerism, using the techniques outlined by Elliotson, in order to render his patient insensible to pain. The attempt was completely successful. The man became profoundly superconscious and completely analgesic. Encouraged, Esdaile experimented further, and shortly thereafter he reported seventy-five painless mesmeric operations to his medical board. Receiving no reply, he sent the results of his operations, by now numbering more than one hundred, to the deputy governor of Bengal. As a consequence, in 1846 he was placed in charge of a hospital in Calcutta.

Esdaile went on to perform several thousand minor and about three hundred major operations, using mesmerism to induce somnambulism and analgesia. These included nineteen amputations. Most, however, were for the removal of gigantic scrotal tumors, the largest of which weighed 103 pounds.[10] The removal of scrotal tumors was considered so dangerous that most surgeons refused to attempt it, and the mortality rate was fifty percent. In 161 consecutive such cases Esdaile's mortality rate was five percent, and all of the deaths occured considerably later from infection or similar causes rather than from shock trauma during or immediately following the operation.

THE SUPERCONSCIOUS WORLD

Like Elliotson before him, Esdaile encountered numb-minded skeptics who insisted that his patients were shamming. He countered this by offering two possible explanations of why increased numbers of patients continued coming to him at the hospital:[11] "I see two ways only of accounting for it; my patients on returning home either say to their friends similarly afflicted, 'What a soft man the doctor is! He cut me to pieces for twenty minutes and I made him believe that I did not feel it. Isn't it a capital joke? Do go and play him the same trick.' Or they may say to their brother sufferers, 'Look at me; I have got rid of my burden . . . . This, I assure you, the doctor did when I was asleep, and I knew nothing about it.' "

Esdaile induced anesthesia in his patients. What is not known is whether he did so by direct suggestion, or whether he merely suggested "sleep" and the patient induced anesthesia himself as a result of believing that it was expected. Today, on the rare occasions when hypnosis is used as a substitute for chemical anesthesia, direct suggestion is used; but it would not be necessary if the subject was already conditioned to believe that anesthesia inevitably accompanied superconsciousness.

Leaving India in 1851 and returning to his native Scotland, Esdaile wrote a year later to Elliotson that he had found the inhabitants of Scotland as susceptible to mesmerism as those of India.[12] Esdaile's successor at the Calcutta hospital, in a lecture at the Medical College, described his predecessor's practice:[13]

> Performing the most dreadful operations of surgery without pain to the patient, must be regarded as the greatest medical triumph of our day. I cannot recall without astonishment the extirpation of a cancerous eye, while the man looked at me unflinching with the other one.

In the light of the testimony of Esdaile's successes, one is tempted to wonder how such solid evidence for the validity of somnambulistic anesthesia could have been denied. But as with his mentor, Elliotson, Esdaile also was incapable of separating science from superstition, and his valid writings were thus similarly tainted. In 1852 he published in London a book titled, *Natural and Mesmeric Clairvoyance, with the practical*

Application of Mesmerism in Surgery and Medicine. Only a small portion of that book was devoted to Esdaile's fanciful belief that certain people could be clairvoyant, either naturally so or while mesmerized, and thus be able to produce an effect (description of an event) that preceded its cause (the event described). But that small portion was quite sufficient to damn his scientific credibility and discredit everything else he had written.

Esdaile was the last of the great mesmerists, that is, proponents of Mesmer's "magnetic fluid" theory. A full twelve years after the publication of Braid's hypnotism book, Esdaile was still arguing:[14]

> It is a *non sequitur* to maintain that, because many of the mesmeric phenomena can be produced by the effects of imagination and suggestion, *therefore* there is no such thing as an independent mesmeric power in nature. From all that has come under my observation, I am convinced, on the contrary, that mesmerism, *as practised by me,* is a physical power exerted by one animal over another . . . and I should as soon adopt the *diabolical* theory as a satisfactory solution of the problem, as attempt to account for what I have seen and done by the action of the imagination alone.

While we can admire the man's will to fight for his beliefs, we must also recognize that Esdaile was completely wrong; and the man who had already spelled out the evidence that he was wrong was a fellow Scotsman, physician James Braid.

Braid first encountered mesmerism when he watched a performance by a Swiss magnetizer named Lafontaine in Manchester in 1841. He was not favorably impressed, and assumed that Lafontaine was a charlatan who used trained stooges. However, he was curious to see more, and returned a week later. At that time he thought he saw some evidence that the mesmeric trance was genuine rather than simulated; but he also saw no evidence of any magnetic fluid. He wondered if a kind of exhaustion due to exertion of the eye muscles in following the mesmerist's "passes" might be the true explanation of the induced sleep.

Braid put his theory to the test. He persuaded a friend to sit and stare at the neck of a wine bottle, and he found that in about three minutes the friend's eyes closed, tears flowed freely, and his head fell forward. Soon after that, he sighed and fell into a deep sleep.

Trying a second experiment, Braid asked his wife to fix her gaze, not on the neck of a wine bottle but on the decoration on a porcelain sugar bowl. The result was the same.

As a final test of his conviction that no physical force from the operator to the subject was involved, Braid instructed his subject that he was to sit and gaze at the designated object after Braid left the room. Braid departed, and returned to find the subject asleep. Further experimentation showed him that eye strain was also not paramount and was in fact detrimental to superconscious induction. He finally found that the most effective method of inducing the superconscious state was to place the object on which the subject was to focus about twelve inches in front of his eyes. That method remains popular with many therapists today.

With the discovery that simple suggestion — not magnetism, not nervous exhaustion, not a dominating personality (although the latter may help) — induced "nervous sleep," Braid made the breakthrough that set Mesmer's discovery on solid scientific ground and shattered the erroneous theories previously used to explain it. In 1843 Braid published *Neurypnology of the Rationale of Nervous Sleep*, in which he introduced the new name, hypnotism, from the Greek *hypnos*, sleep, in order to supplant the discredited mesmerism and the clearly erroneous magnetism. Later he would try to abolish that name also, when he discovered that the superconscious state was not in fact any form of sleep. But Braid's very success in separating hypnotism from the unscientific beliefs of the mesmerists, guaranteed that the new word would outlive its creator.

Even though Braid was not the first to recognize the role of suggestion in bringing about the superconscious state, it was he who spelled out the full implication of that recognition. The most expert hypnotist, he asserted, could achieve nothing if the subject was given no knowledge of what was expected of him. While continually gazing at a point of focus might tire a person and induce sleep even when the subject was unaware that he was *expected* to fall asleep, anesthesia could not occur unless, directly or indirectly, the subject had been taught to expect such a condition. The most effective means of inducing hypnosis was direct suggestion; physical means — whether aids to concentration or pure mumbo jumbo — were only effective when they carried the implied suggestion, "This is going to work."

Braid made the most important discovery, without which modern hypnotherapy would be impractical. He discovered that all major symptoms of hypnotism — catalepsy, anesthesia, amnesia — could be induced without sleep. Sleep was therefore not the basis of hypnotism but merely another symptom. It was at that point that he tried, unsuccessfully, to replace the word hypnotism with "monoideaism." Since one of the beneficial symptoms of the superconscious state is the curing of nervous habits, Braid in effect revealed to the world that superconscious treatment of such habits was practical, not only for the five percent who can achieve the deepest sleep-like condition, but also for the ninety-five percent capable of focusing their minds on a therapist's live or recorded voice.

Braid was an insightful man who stripped away the nonsense previously believed about the superconscious state. But he was also a product of his time and, despite his unquestioned brilliance as a scientist, he could not avoid falling victim to the currently fashionable nonsense belief of phrenology.

Braid believed that if certain bumps on a subject's head were pressed while he was superconscious, predetermined behaviour could be elicited. For example, if the "veneration" bump was pressed, the subject would assume the kneeling, hands-pressed position of a worshipper in church. Braid tested his theory — and found that it was correct.

In Braid's writings, we are not told how the information was conveyed to the subject or what was expected of him; but we can be very sure the information *was* conveyed. Replication of Braid's phrenology tests on patients *not* conditioned to expect such a result produced no such behaviour. It is difficult, in retrospect, to understand how Braid could have failed to detect in his own experiments the same "dirty test tube" effect he had discerned in others. Nonetheless, fortunately for Braid the tremendous value of his main discovery was able to override, and enable later scientists to overlook, his one published lapse into self-delusion.

THE SUPERCONSCIOUS WORLD

After Braid, the research and work of Liebeault and Bernheim at Nancy and Charcot at Salpetriere merely enlarged upon and spread out from what was already known. The three contributed more to making hypnotism respectable than to an increase in knowledge. Many later researchers expanded and refined that knowledge, but among hypnotists no later contribution superseded Braid's.

The man who did advance superconscious theory to a level that threw doubt on the hypnotists' dogmatic adherence to the notion of a trance state, was Emile Coué. Coué maintained that the assumption of a trance-like state was itself a response to a direct or implied suggestion, and any therapeutic result that could be obtained by inducing a trance could be equally well accomplished with a subject indisputably awake. Not surprisingly, the hypnotic fraternity tends to exclude Coué from its canon of pioneers, and some histories of the development of hypnotism fail to mention him at all.

Coué was a pharmacist whose experiments with suggestion date from two brief meetings that he had with Liebeault. Coué's first attempts to hypnotize, using Liebeault's methods, failed, and this led him (as it would lead Sigmund Freud, for the same reason) to seek an alternative means of obtaining the same result. But whereas Freud came up with a methodology that was patently valueless, Coué went on to invent an auto-suggestion theory that foreshadowed my own theory of superconsciousness.

Coué was the first person to realize that all effective suggestion is auto-suggestion. It is not self-evidently so. A medical man who witnessed one of Coué's demonstrations remarked, "There is no *auto*-suggestion in it; it is all *Coué*-suggestion." [15] Coué's answer was, "You make a suggestion to someone; if the unconscious of the latter does not accept it, in order to transform it into auto-suggestion, it produces no result." [16]

When Coué's answer is applied to superconscious terminology, its parallel with my own thinking becomes evident: A suggestion is given. That suggestion is intercepted and evaluated by the watchdog. If the watchdog accepts the suggestion as non-harmful, the imagination then reacts as if the suggestion is an acceptable fact. Coué, incidentally, is the author of that great positive suggestion, "Day by day, in every way, I am getting better and better."

THE SUPERCONSCIOUS WORLD

No new or significant use of suggestion really supersedes the discoveries of Coué. Indeed, the most publicized research into superconscious phenomena during the past fifty years has been devoted to proving hypotheses that are *not* true.

And that leads into the subject of the next, and I suspect most controversial, chapter.

CHAPTER FIVE

SUPERCONSCIOUS LIFE REGRESSION

The mid-1950s was an exciting time to be a practitioner of hypnotism. Newspapers and radio stations throughout Australia (television was still a year away) were headlining the "fact" that hypnotism had supplied proof that we have lived before. A young Pueblo, Colorado, housewife named Ruth Simmons had, in several hypnotic sessions since 1952, revealed her previous existence and described her life as Bridey Murphy, a woman born in Ireland at the end of the eighteenth century. The hypnotist responsible for bringing this startling revelation to the world's attention was a business man and amateur hypnotist, Morey Bernstein. With the publication of Bernstein's book, *The Search for Bridey Murphy*, in 1956, the reincarnation craze among hypnotists began and has not yet abated.

Bernstein, who had used hypnotism previously to help friends overcome nervous habits, decided that:[1]

> Tonight I will attempt an experiment in hypnosis that I have never before undertaken. The subject will be Ruth Simmons. This is November 29, 1952 . . . . For this particular purpose, I knew, I must have a splendid subject. This would be old stuff for Ruth Simmons; with me as hypnotist she had done the same thing twice before . . . . She had shown conclusively that she could, while hypnotized, recall events which had taken place when she was only one year old. But tonight I was going to attempt

something more than an ordinary age regression. This time I would learn just how far back her memory could be taken.... It took only a few minutes to hypnotize her.

Besides Bernstein, the witnesses of this historic session were Bernstein's wife, Hazel, and Ruth's husband, Rex, as Bernstein named them. In fact Ruth was a pseudonym used in the book and initial press reports. Her real name was Virginia Tighe.

Bernstein continued:[2]

> As soon as I was satisfied that the trance was sufficiently deep, I turned on the tape recorder and began speaking quietly.... "Now we are going to turn back through time and space, just like turning back the pages of a book .... And when I next talk to you, you will be seven years old."... Finally I asked, "Do you go to school?" Her voice came, clear and small as she answered my questions....
> "Who sits in front of you?"
> "Jacqueline."
> "And who sits behind you?"
> "Verna Mae."
> In the same way Ruth returned to her kindergarten days, when she was five years old.... Then Ruth at the age of three... gave an elaborate description of her colored doll.... Farther and farther we went... until Ruth remembered when she was only one year old.... And now — now at last... I was ready... to take her "over the hump".... I was going to make an effort to determine whether human memory can be taken back to a period even before birth.
> I instructed the entranced Mrs. Simmons... that she should try to go still further back in her memory... "back, back, back and back... until, oddly enough, you find yourself in some other scene, in some other place, in some other time, and when I talk to you again, you will tell me about it."... I asked her name, the answer came... "Friday... Friday Murphy."

(I was under the impression that she had said "Friday." The others in the room, as they later told me, also thought she said "Friday". But we were soon to learn otherwise.)
"Why did they name you Friday?"
"Bridey . . . Bridey."
"Oh, I see. Bridey. Why did they name you that?"
"Named me after my grandmother, Bridget . . . 'n' I'm Bridey."

Virginia Tighe's responses were spoken in a soft Irish brogue. In that and five subsequent taped sessions she declared that she was born in Cork in 1798 and that she died in 1864. She was the daughter of a Protestant barrister, Duncan Murphy, and at the age of twenty she married a Catholic barrister, Brian MacCarthy. She was married first in a Protestant ceremony in Cork and then a Catholic ceremony in Belfast. She lived after her marriage on Dooley Road, Belfast, and in 1847, or later, Brian taught at Queen's University. Additional information brought forward included the name of the priest, John Gorman, who allegedly performed her Catholic marriage.

What made the Bridey Murphy case so appealing to the world was its very ordinariness. Not only was Bridey herself an ordinary person, completely unknown to history, but she was also unacquainted with any famous people or important events. Given that the great majority of people are ordinary, the probability of an insignificant housewife being equally unknown in a previous life was overwhelming. The fact that Bridey Murphy was ordinary gave the case credibility. So popular did Bridey become, that Bob Hope was able to joke about a millionaire who died and left everything to himself.

Historians made the first dent in the Bridey Murphy tale by pointing out that the Ireland described by Bridey existed not in history but in popular fantasy. No trace could be found of any Dooley Road in nineteenth-century Belfast. Nor could the existence of a Brian MacCarthy of Queen's University, or a priest named John Gorman, be verified. A couple of details did check out, however. Two grocers whom Bridey had mentioned were indeed listed in a Belfast city directory for 1865-6.

THE SUPERCONSCIOUS WORLD

It was the *Chicago American*, less than six months after the publication of Bernstein's book, that annihilated the theory that the source of Tighe's Bridey Murphy tale was a previous incarnation. Tighe was discovered to have had an Irish aunt who had regaled the young Virginia with tales of old Ireland. And when Virginia had lived in Chicago as a child, the house across the street from her was occupied by an Irish woman — named Bridey Murphy!

There was no nineteenth-century Bridey Murphy. There was only a twentieth-century Bridey Murphy, whom Virginia Tighe met as a child and then forgot. The information Tighe dredged out of her mind under hypnosis had been impressed there when she was a child. This of course raises the question: Why did Virginia Tighe use information from her childhood to pretend that she had lived before in another country as another person in another body? Was the whole Bridey Murphy tale a hoax?

Some past-lives phenomena undoubtedly *are* hoaxes. Shortly after the Bridey Murphy publicity, an Australian hypnotist appeared on television in both Melbourne and Sydney and had a subject recount a past life in which she spoke fluent Russian. What the hypnotist did not mention to his viewers was that the girl's first language in her present life was also Russian.

In Morey Bernstein's case, however, I see no reason to doubt that he acted in good faith. Nor do I question that Virginia Tighe was genuinely superconscious when she became Bridey Murphy, or that she genuinely remembered nothing of her Bridey Murphy story when awakened. How can that be, you ask? Let me explain.

Superconscious subjects are highly suggestible. To refuse a trusted operator's instruction, they would need a very strong reason related to their deep-rooted beliefs. When Bernstein ordered Tighe to recount a past life, that order did not in any way conflict with her moral, ethical or religious beliefs. She therefore had no reason to refuse to obey it. There is a further consideration. A hypnotist is very much an authority figure, and commands the same kind of respect and awe (at least in the eyes of persons who choose to become his subjects) as a doctor or a teacher. The subject therefore feels a strong inner compulsion to please the operator — within the limits set by the watchdog. Impelled to obey Bernstein's instruction to *relive* a past life, Virginia Tighe complied the only way she was able: by *inventing* a past life, utilizing whatever information was available in the recesses of her memory.

I had the fortunate experience of having this theory completely confirmed in front of several thousand listeners to a national radio program presented by the Canadian Broadcasting Corporation in 1969. The program was "Cross Canada Check-up," and ran for two hours on Sunday afternoons. It was hosted by two moderators from the national press, and listeners were invited to phone in, collect, from anywhere in North America, and question or debate guests on the topic under discussion.

Early in the second hour, the moderators led me into a discussion of the questions surrounding reincarnation and the feasibility of the Bridey Murphy case. I gave an almost identical answer to the explanation above. One of the moderators then smiled and informed me that they had traced the woman who had been Bridey Murphy and that she had been listening to my answer on the telephone and was standing by to add her comments. Her name since remarrying was Virginia Morrow. She was asked what were her thoughts on my explanation, and she answered, "I agree with Mr. Reveen one hundred percent. I do not believe I have lived before, and anything I brought forward was from family memories."

The Bridey Murphy case was not a hoax. It was, however, a classic example of how the public *is* hoaxed on a regular basis by the mass media. I was, as mentioned, in Australia when *The Search for Bridey Murphy* was published. In every newspaper and on every radio station I learned that proof was finally forthcoming that we have lived before. Yet at no time did I ever learn from those same newspapers or radio stations that the true source of Tighe's Bridey Murphy memories had been discovered, and it was not any past life. The media rationalize that "reincarnation is news" and "not-reincarnation is not news." Rubbish. Giving extensive coverage to sensationalized nonsense, and little or no coverage to rebuttals of that nonsense, makes the media morally culpable for the public's continued belief in dozens of theories and superstitions that have in fact been fully refuted by competent research.[3]

The Bridey Murphy case was a Pandora's box that, once opened, could not be closed. Hypnotists everywhere ordered their subjects to recount past lives and — guess what? — they did so. In Britain hypnotherapist Arnall Bloxham taped interviews with more than four hundred subjects who, on command, obediently described past lives. Television producer Jeffrey Iverson learned of Bloxham's experiments and turned them into a television program for the BBC. That program, twenty years after the discovery that Bridey Murphy was *not* a past life, made no mention of the possibility that past lives were merely superconscious dreams — another instance of a powerful arm of the media giving a one-sided sensationalist view of a many-faceted subject. Iverson then wrote a book about Bloxham's cases,[4] that likewise omitted any mention of superconscious subjects' proven ability to fantasize.

Bloxham's most impressive case involved a subject whom he pseudonymously called Jane Evans. Jane described six past lives, including a tutor's wife in third-century Britain, a Jewish woman in twelfth-century York, an Egyptian-born courtesan in fifteenth-century France, a sixteenth-century Spanish maidservant, a sewing wench in eighteenth-century London, and a nineteenth-century American nun. And each regression was accompanied by an enormous amount of detail, including a wealth of personal and place names consistent with the relevant period. Consider the following passage:[5]

> We are on our way to Verulum. The *domina*, Constantine, Favonius, Hilary and Vitus . . . . I knew we shouldn't trust Allectus — when Constantius had sailed for Rome, Carausius brought the fleet over. He landed and he has conquered Britain — Carausius has come over and he has taken over and we have had to flee — Allectus came to our house — killed some of our servants — but Favonius managed to kill some of Allectus's men and we have had to go by dark. We are going to Verulum . . . . *domina* Helena said we had to escape . . . . if they know that Constantius's wife and son, Constantine, are in Verulum, they will come for us . . . . I didn't like Allectus . . . . And now Carausius rules Britain.

The narrator of that tale was Jane Evans' earliest imagined incarnation, Livonia, wife of Titus, tutor to an aristocratic Roman family. And while Livonia herself was not a person whose existence can be verified (or disproven), the family she worked for was rather more famous.

The *Constantius* referred to was Aurelius Valerius Constantius, military governor of Britain in the late third century. His wife, the *domina* ("Lady") Helena, was the woman canonized as Saint Helena. Their son Constantine was the first Christian emperor, a fact of which Jane Evans seemed unaware, since she was describing a time prior to Constantine's elevation to the purple. Carausius and Allectus are the persons who illicitly seized power when Constantius left for Rome in 286. Verulum was the Roman name for St. Albans, just as Eboracum, the name Livonia consistently used, was the Roman name for York.

The Livonia case was most impressive, since a good deal of the historical information Jane Evans recited was verifiable and turned out to be correct. Also, while the availability of sources of verification means that Evans could have read the information and forgotten it, historian Brian Hartley stated, "She knew some quite remarkable historical facts, and numerous published works would have to be consulted if anyone tried to prepare the outline of such a story."[6] And while much of Livonia's information covered periods in the principals' lives for which no records survive, for that very reason it could not be falsified.

I have cited the above case in some detail, to show that many past-life regressions indeed sound plausible and do not always contain detectable errors or inconsistencies. And Jane Evans' filling in details from the dark (unknown) periods of her characters' lives was as plausible and consistent as the guesses of the most skilled writers of historical novels.

There was, however, one significant inconsistency. While English-language history books invariably refer to Constantius, Carausius and Allectus by their Roman names, I have never personally encountered any that referred to the Emperor Constantinius by any name but the anglicized "Constantine." Jane Evans referred throughout to the future Roman emperor, not by the name that a historical Livonia would have known him, but by the only name Jane Evans would have encountered in her reading. More to the point, Jane Evans' Livonia referred to Constantinius by the anglicized name used by author Louis De Wohl in his 1947 historical novel, *The Living Wood.*

THE SUPERCONSCIOUS WORLD

Every single piece of information given by Livonia can be traced to De Wohl's novel. The claim that, in effect, only a history buff could have accumulated so much information, and only by research involving a large number of sources, was correct — but the researcher was not Jane Evans; it was Louis De Wohl. And whereas the coincidence of De Wohl's novel containing all of Evans' factual information shows only that the novel *could have* been Evans' source, a more startling parallel shows that it *was* the source.

Not only did Livonia refer to historical persons who all appeared in *The Living Wood*; her superconscious fantasy also included De Wohl's *fictitious* characters, Curio and Valerius.[7] And as a wise man from the east once wrote, "Evidence that is discredited in part is discredited entirely."

As impressive as Jane Evans' Livonia was for its abundance of verifiable detail, her Rebecca was more so. Rebecca was the wife of a wealthy Jew in twelfth-century York. She described being pursued through the streets by an anti-Semitic mob, hiding in the crypt of a church, and being found and lynched.

A massacre of Jews did take place in York in March, 1190. The fact of the massacre was widely known, and Jane Evans' awareness of it cannot be deemed significant. However, based on Jane's general description of the church in which Rebecca hid, a historian tentatively identified it as St. Mary's Castlegate. Rebecca had allegedly hidden in a crypt, and St. Mary's was thought to have lacked a crypt. Then in September 1975, long after Rebecca had taped her story, workmen converting St. Mary's into a museum unearthed evidence of an undatable but possibly recent charnel vault that believers promptly dubbed a "crypt."

To this day, Jane Evans' Rebecca continues to be cited as the strongest evidence for the reality of reincarnation. For the first time, a superconscious subject had provided information that she could not have learned, since no record of it existed, but which could nonetheless be verified afterwards. All previous cases had involved the "chicken or egg" dilemma: If no record survived, the information could never be verified. Yet if any historical record, however obscure, did exist, then it was always possible that, somehow, the subject had managed to learn its contents. Rebecca had at last provided unlearned, accurate information. Reincarnationists were jubilant.

Unfortunately for its proponents, the Rebecca case is far less impressive on closer examination. In the first place, since most people expected old English churches to have crypts, it was by no means improbable that Rebecca would have imagined a church with a crypt. And when it turned out that St. Mary's indeed had a crypt, that too could be mere coincidence. But the strongest rebuttal of the St. Mary's crypt prediction was that twelfth-century York had more than forty churches, and since Rebecca did not name the church in which she hid, its identification by a believer as St. Mary's Castlegate was sheer speculation. In fact, when Rebecca's church was narrowed down to three most probables, St. Mary's was chosen for use in Iverson's television program because it was the most accessible!

There were other weaknesses in the Rebecca story. She consistently referred to Coppergate as an actual gate. Yet in the twelfth century there was no such gate; Coppergate was merely the name of a street. And she referred to Coney Street, when in the twelfth century it was still known only as Cuninga Street. But those weaknesses were not too serious if taken alone. Far more definitive were the anachronisms that follow.

Rebecca repeated four times that Jews of the period were required to wear yellow badges, "circles over our hearts." But the imposition of identifying badges on Jews did not begin until the following century, and even then the English badge consisted of two white strips that represented the tablets of Moses. The yellow circle was used to identify Jews in France and Germany, not England, and only after 1215.

Rebecca described her home as being in a ghetto, a Jewish area in North York. But there was never a Jewish quarter in York. Jews lived scattered among the Christians. And the word *ghetto*, derived from the Italian *geto* — "foundry" — did not come into existence until the establishment of the *first* ghetto, on a foundry site, in 1516.

Jane Evans brought together information and vocabulary from later periods to augment her life of Rebecca. Two of her other "past lives" can be traced to specific historical novels, *The Living Wood* and C.B. Costain's *The Moneyman*.[8] As for her other sources: Since Jane Evans is a pseudonym, and Bloxham refuses to reveal her true identity, there is the obvious problem that her youthful reading habits and knowledge of York, where two of her past-life fantasies were located, cannot be investigated.

The weaknesses in the Rebecca story discredit the claim that this is a case of proven reincarnation. Weaknesses in some of Bloxham's other subjects' stories are more pronounced. For example, a subject claiming to be an Iriqui (presumably Iriquois) related tales that he had heard from "the Coast Indians" — four centuries before Columbus made the mistake of calling the American natives "Indians." He claimed to have witnessed a Viking invasion, and described the horned helmets always seen in movies, but in Viking history helmets were worn only in religious rituals and only by men of rank. He used Hollywood-Indian speech: "Wise men say, if you hit the part that pumps the blood, deer will die straightaway."[9]

The subject's concept of an eleventh-century American native apparently had no word for heart, even though men who hunted deer for food were unquestionably familiar with such an organ. Yet he had the concept "pump" five centuries before such a device was first seen in North America, and was aware that the heart is a pump six centuries before Harvey discovered the circulation of the blood.

The most notable inconsistency in past-life regressions is the prevalence of anachronisms. Bloxham's pre-Columbian Indian was familiar with the circulation of the blood and Columbus's equation of Americans with Indians. Bernstein's Bridey Murphy used twentieth-century Americanisms, such as candy, downtown, and school (meaning college) unknown in nineteenth-century Ireland. A subject of Harry Hurst described a past life in the Thebes of Pharaoh Ramses III, long before historians retroactively gave pharoahs numbers to distinguish them from other pharoahs of the same name, and long before the Greeks ever referred to No-Amun as Thebai and English translators rendered Thebai as Thebes.[10]

By far the most interesting and informative example of how a superconscious mind is able to create past lives out of information that has seemingly been totally forgotten, is the case of one of the subjects of Canadian hypnotist Dr. Harold Rosen. When regressed to a past life, Rosen's subject wrote a passage in a strange script that neither he nor Rosen could identify as either a legitimate language or known alphabet.

On investigation it was discovered that the subject had written a passage in Oscan, a language spoken in western Italy prior to the first century BC, at which time it was superseded by Latin. The passage was an accurate transcription of the "Curse of Vibria," a fifth-century BC leaden scroll buried with a dead Oscan to guide him through the underworld. The subject declared that he had never studied Latin and had never even heard of Oscan.

Rosen, not being a believer in reincarnation, rendered the subject superconscious again and instructed him to regress in his mind to the time when he first encountered the Oscan curse. The subject promptly declared that he was sitting in a library alongside a person studying an open book in which the Oscan curse was on an upturned page. The subject had merely glanced at the page, and no detail had impressed itself on his conscious awareness. But the entire passage had nonetheless been photographically imprinted into his memory, and under superconsciousness he was able to recollect it and utilize it to fulfill an instruction to relive an (imagined) past life.[11]

Dozens of past lives recounted while superconscious have been investigated and found to be fantasies based on information learned in *this* life. That does not prove that all past-life descriptions are fantasies; but it does prove that a superconscious subject, told to relive a past life, is able to comply convincingly by fantasizing. If all experimenters in this field would only follow Dr. Rosen's scientific approach and ask their subjects to go back to the time when they first learned information brought forward in a past-life fantasy, and reveal the source of that knowledge, I have no doubt that the results would prove to be more mundane than sensational. But I seriously doubt that the BBC would then be interested in doing a three-part series based on such results.

There is a standard procedure in scientific research called *reductio ad absurdum*, in which a hypothesis is tested by assuming that it is true, and then examining the consequences of that assumption. Let us therefore assume, not that reincarnation is real, but merely that a majority of past lives recounted while superconscious are genuine memories of pre-birth experiences. Where does such an assumption lead?

The first logical expectation would be that any pattern in past-life geography and chronology must exist independently of the operator or hypnotist performing the regression. For example, we might find that all rebirths occur approximately nine months after the previous death; or we might find that months, years, even centuries elapse between incarnations; or we might find a random pattern, with some subjects reborn immediately, others having long periods between incarnations, and still others having no interval between some lives and long intervals between others. What we will *not* find if the past lives are genuine, is all subjects regressed by hypnotist "A" having continuous incarnations with approximately nine months between them, while all who are regressed by hypnotist "B" have centuries between incarnations.

Similarly we might expect individuals to have all of their incarnations in the same geographic area, or to span the globe, or a combination of the two. We would *not* expect to find that all subjects of hypnotist "A" were reborn somewhere in the same country; all subjects of hypnotist "B" were reborn within an hour's walk of where they died; and all subjects of hypnotist "C" had past lives that covered the whole planet. If we did uncover such improbable correlations, we would be obliged to conclude that the subjects were recounting, not past-life patterns that had actually befallen them, but past-life patterns that they knew the particular hypnotist expected of them.

In fact we do find that, both chronologically and geographically, subjects' past-life recollections tend to conform very closely to the expectations of the involved hypnotist. In geographic areas where reincarnation is a facet of the dominant religion (e.g., India), patterns conform to the local cultural expectation.

For example, of thirty-seven reincarnation claims investigated by Dr. Ian Stevenson, mostly in India and Alaska, the longest interval between death and rebirth was nineteen years and the second-longest nine years. Excluding the case in which an Indian claimed to be the reincarnation of a person who had not died until his alleged reincarnation was three years old, the shortest was four months. Of the thirty-seven, one was reborn three hundred miles from where he died; seven between fifty and one hundred miles away; and the rest (except for a Sri Lankan who claimed to have been an Englishman in his preceding life) less than fifty miles away.[12] Stevenson was not a hypnotist. He was merely an investigator who examined cases in which very young children claimed to have memories of being another person who had recently died a short distance away. However, what makes his studies relevant is that many persons regard his data as the strongest evidence yet produced for the reality of reincarnation. Unfortunately it does not survive inspection.

A reinvestigation of Stevenson's reported Indian cases revealed that reincarnation claims by children had significantly increased the tourist trade in those areas where such claims were common, and had become somewhat of a cottage industry. In one case a child claimed to be the dead son of a nearby rich man and asked to be recognized as his past-life father's heir. However, when his past-life father suffered a financial reversal, while his current father's standing increased, he withdrew his claim. And in several instances children claiming past-life memories were found to have been coached by their parents for the titillation of gullible western journalists and actresses.[12]

Stevenson's pattern of short distances and short times between incarnations is repeated in the regressions performed by English hypnotist Joe Keeton. While Keeton finds exceptions, whom he dismisses as "Walter Mittys," the bulk of his nine thousand past-life regressions conform precisely to his personal expectation and belief that the transition from death to conception is instantaneous. Keeton's subjects are all reborn nine months after their previous deaths. They also conform to his expectation that an English person's previous lives will all have been in England. Apparently the gulf between genteel Englishmen and mere foreigners is unbridgeable, even for transmigrating souls.

The subjects of the less insular Arnall Bloxham, in contrast, show a wide diversity in the geography and chronology of their past lives, a diversity that is repeated among the subjects of California hypnotist Dr. Helen Wambach. As an examination of the various researchers' own books will confirm,[13] the geographical and chronological patterns of the cases charted below are typical of the bulk of all cases of the specific investigator reporting them.

As the charts show, patterns found in one hypnotist's life regressions, or in an area of India where reincarnation is fashionable, do not occur

THE SUPERCONSCIOUS WORLD

Hypnotist: Arnall Bloxham
unidentified subject: a housewife

TIME	PLACE	STATUS
present	Wales	housewife
time of Philip of Navarre	Spain	Spaniard, male
sixteenth century	Peru	Inca priest
? medieval	Bavaria England	count's son female witch
?	Europe	steward's son
? Roman era	China Rome	? charioteer, male
classical age	Athens	governor's daughter
time of Ramses II	Egypt	trader's wife

Hypnotist: Helen Wambach
subject: R. Logg, San Francisco

TIME	PLACE	STATUS
1900-02	Baltimore	girl
1870	London	cabin boy
1810-70	Egypt	supervisor, male
1715-90	England	businessman
?	France	peasant
1590-1618	Wales	unmarried mother
1500s	Italy	nobleman
400 BC	Egypt	merchant, female
1300 BC	Egypt	driver, male
2000 BC	Egypt	high priest

Hypnotist: Joe Keeton
subject: Edna Greena

TIME	PLACE	STATUS
1927 - present	Lancs.	housewife
1850-1926	Lancs.	washerwoman
1780-1850	Plymouth	housewife
died 1779	Lincoln	woman
born 1688	England	vagrant, male
1650-87	London	Nell Gwynn
1613-49 executed 1612	London Lancs.	woman witch

Investigator: Ian Stevenson
subjects: children claiming one past life

DIED	BORN	DISTANCE APART
Apr. 1950	Aug. 1951	6 miles
Jan. 1948	Mar. 1954	11 miles
Jan. 1951	July 1951	half mile
May 1943	Oct. 1944	90 miles
Apr. 1951	Oct. 1959	22 miles
Oct. 1922	Mar. 1923	300 miles
Feb. 1953	Aug. 1962	10 miles
Apr. 1964	Aug. 1964	10 miles
May 1954	1950 |sic		20 miles

(based on charts in Wilson, *Mind Out of Time*)

among subjects of another hypnotist or in an area where reincarnation is at best a fringe belief. As Ian Wilson comments:[14]

> The observation can scarcely be escaped that the subjects of regression experiments, without any overt priming by the hypnotists, subtly and chameleon-like seem to reflect in their past lives the expectations held by the man who has hypnotized them. At the very least, the suggestion is disquieting.

Subjects of past-life regressions perform as the involved operator expects. They demonstrate inconsistencies and anachronisms. And in many cases they reveal an ignorance of facts that the alleged past-life personality would definitely know.

For example, Joe Keeton's subject Sue Atkins in one of her incarnations became a Jesuit priest, Father Antony Bennet, born about 1637 and living through the reign of Charles II. Father Bennet attended a Jesuit seminary in Rome. Yet when Sue Atkins, in her Father Bennet persona, was asked by psychologist Hans Eysenck to recite her Latin prayers, the result was, in Eysenck's words:[15]

> Father Antony never got beyond the first two words of *Pater noster*. The notion that a Jesuit priest who had been to Rome could not say a Latin prayer is of course preposterous, and that he would not know his *Pater noster* is beyond belief.

In my own concerts I occasionally demonstrate past-life regression for my audience's entertainment, always explaining that they are *not* seeing evidence for the reality of reincarnation. In one show I had two men at the same time both claiming to be King Henry VIII of England. Clearly, for either one to be recalling a genuine former incarnation, the other must have been fantasizing. Another time I had two subjects, a man and a woman, both claiming to be Christopher Columbus. And once, in 1985, I even had a subject regress to a past life in which he was Prince Charles, husband of Diana and son of Queen Elizabeth II. At least he was younger than the real Prince Charles , who is still alive and in good health at the time of writing.

THE SUPERCONSCIOUS WORLD

Quite often, to make the demonstration more entertaining for my audience, I tell my volunteers in life-regression demonstrations that they will recount their experiences from a time when they were closely involved with significant persons or events from history. Since for every person with a close involvement with the great events of history there are thousands with no such involvement, most subjects would, despite my instructions, be obliged to recount past lives as "nobodies" — if the past-life memory was genuine. Yet the subjects always obediently identify themselves as the kind of "somebody" I had suggested they should be. Why? Because I indicated my expectations, and they accordingly conformed to those expectations.

The correlation between the operator's expectations and the results of past-life regressions was graphically demonstrated in a recent experiment by University of Kentucky psychologist, Robert A. Baker.[16] Sixty subjects were utilized who had proven to be equally susceptible to superconscious suggestion, and they were randomly divided into three groups of twenty each.

Group A was told (paraphrased):

> There is a dramatic new form of therapy being used by many Californian doctors. They take a patient back under hypnosis to his former lives, and find the traumatic event in one of those lives that is the cause of neurosis in his present life. We are going to take you back, and some of you will probably experience more past lives than one.

Group B was told:

> There is a new therapy in California which purports to be able to take a person back, under hypnosis, to a past life. The theory behind it may or may not be true; but today I'm going to try it with all of you. Some of you might experience a past life. Who knows?

Group C was in effect told:

There is a lunatic fringe in California who claim to be able to treat people by hypnotizing them into recalling past lives. It sounds ridiculous, but let's see if any of you will be able to bring forward a past life. Frankly I don't believe a word of it.

All three groups were then given identical instructions to regress under superconsciousness to a time long before they were born and to tell the experimenter who and where they were. In group A, seventeen of the twenty dutifully described at least one past life, and fifteen of them described two or more past lives. In group B, twelve responded with at least one past life, and nine of them recounted more than one. But in group C, only two out of twenty produced a past life, and both were found afterwards to belong to religions in which the reality of reincarnation is an article of faith.

If superconscious past-life descriptions are genuine memories of former incarnations, then it must be impossible for subjects' past-life patterns to parallel the beliefs, expectations and whims of the hypnotist who happens to be regressing them. Yet we have seen just such a correlation between suggested or implied expectations and results. Since genuine past-life memories could not produce such correlations, clearly some factor other than reincarnation must be responsible for the observed results.

All that has been demonstrated so far is that reincarnation has never been shown to exist through superconscious life regression. Hypnotists who regard reincarnation as a proven fact are therefore self-deluded. It has not, however, been proven that reincarnation *does not* exist; nor can this ever be scientifically proven by any experiment. That conclusion can only be philosophically proven. (Scientific proof can show that a conclusion *is* true. Philosophical proof can show only that it *must be* true.)

There are currently five billion human beings on this planet. For reincarnation to exist, with souls transmigrating from body to body, then all five billion must have souls. (The existence of the soul is not an issue here. While I personally believe in the reality of the soul, I would not insult readers of other faiths by presenting a personal religious belief as an axiom. I postulate the existence of a soul purely for the sake of my argument, not because it happens to coincide with my own beliefs.) There

THE SUPERCONSCIOUS WORLD

must therefore be at least five billion souls in existence, not counting any that are currently between incarnations. Yet if we go back a mere three thousand years the population of planet Earth was only a few million. If we go back fifty thousand years, the population was only a few thousand. And if we go back a couple of million years, the hominid population was only a few hundred.

Where were those five billion souls when there were only a few hundred, or a few thousand, or a few million bodies for them to inhabit? The only answer consistent with the assumption that the soul exists and transmigrates from body to body, is that every time the human population doubles or triples, a corresponding number of souls are brought into existence. In practical terms this means that, depending on current birth and death rates, anywhere from one tenth to one half of all newborn babies have new souls that have never occupied any other body.

Yet reincarnation proponents maintain that *all* persons currently alive have lived before. And, when encouraged to do so by positive expectations, *all* superconscious subjects are capable of describing past lives. Clearly something does not add up.

If superconscious past-lives are not reincarnation memories, what are they? One theory that has been put forward is genetic memory. What that means is that memories may be passed on from ancestor to descendant through the genes. That explanation would be plausible except for one thing. Every gene or chromosome passed on from parent to child is identical down to the last atom with a gene or chromosome that the parent possessed from the instant of his/her conception. While we do not yet know how the human brain processes memories (although neurologists may be coming close to finding the answer), we do know that the brain's molecular structure does not remain unchanged from one second to the next. Somehow memory is related to observable changes in the brain.

On the other hand, a gene that remains unchanged from the moment of the parent's conception until its fusion with another cell to form a new life, cannot contain information that had not been there at the beginning of the parent's life. Every gene in the human body is identical with a gene possessed by an ancestor who lived a million years ago. It therefore cannot contain any information of any event since that time — unless that information is contained at a level micro-physics has not yet succeeded in penetrating. We now know that atoms, far from being indivisible, are made up of several identified and perhaps more as-yet-unidentified smaller particles. While two genes may be identical at the atomic level, we cannot be completely certain that they are identical at the sub-atomic level.

The genetic-memory theory finally fails, however, in its inability to explain a superconscious subject's alleged memories of his former self's old age and death. Our ancestors tended to marry and have children at an early age. Self-evidently, memories of a person's later years could not have been genetically transferred to children conceived many years earlier.

We are left with only one explanation consistent with the observable details of all past-life regressions. While I would not presume to tell anyone that he may not believe in reincarnation as an explanation for *some* inexplicable phenomena, it has been clearly shown that, in at least some past-life descriptions, reincarnation is not the answer. There is no doubt that superconscious dreaming is the explanation of most past-life regressions and, that being so, we must recognize it as a possible explanation of all such cases. If reincarnation is to be taken seriously, its proponents must find some better evidence than superconscious regression. So far they have not done so.

CHAPTER SIX

SUPERCONSCIOUS USES AND ABUSES

I have already mentioned the past-life therapy that "lunatic fringe" groups are practising, mainly in California. It would be nice to say that such groups exist only in imaginative fiction, but sadly that is not so. Despite the fact that past-life memories have been shown to be mostly, if not totally, dream fantasies, a new school of hypnoquackery has indeed arisen that depends for its validity on the assumption that reincarnation is a proven fact.

The theory behind past-life therapy is that present-life neuroses, psychoses, phobias, and other irrational behaviour have past-life causes. For example, a white woman suffering from claustrophobia had been a black slavegirl in a previous life, and had been locked in a cramped, windowless hot box when she refused to gratify her owner's sexual demands.[1] A woman suffering from sexual inadequacy had been a prostitute who was verbally and physically abused and castigated for daring to enjoy sexual activity.[2] Acrophobia is caused by falling to one's death in a previous life. Sadistic tendencies are caused by past-life experiences in a culture in which a patrician who did *not* cruelly misuse his slaves and prisoners was considered "queer." Bedwetting is caused by . . . . And so it goes on.

There are two forms of past-life therapy. While they do not themselves use such terms, they might well be divided into the Bridey Murphy and the Sigmund Freud schools. The former uses standard life-regression techniques under superconsciousness. The latter has wide-awake subjects repeat phrases and words relevant to their present problems (shades of Coué) until "free association" causes them to start babbling fantasies that they eventually identify as past lives.

According to a practitioner of the Freudian or free-association school:[3]

> Past-lives therapy does not depend on the truth of reincarnation, but on putting aside the question of truth in order to work toward curing the patient's behavioural problem . . . . As far as my patients are concerned, the success of their therapy is unaffected whether they embrace a belief in reincarnation or remain skeptical throughout.

On the surface, Dr. Netherton's position seems reasonable. If irrational compulsive behaviour, psycho-neurosis, social or physical dysfunction, phobia or mania can be cured by having the patient fantasize a past-life cause, then it is hard to argue with success. It is an observable fact that a psychotic who believes he is "possessed" cannot be cured by a therapist who tries to convince him that the demon possessing him does not exist. Rather, he can only be cured by a therapist who utilizes his delusion and convinces him that his demon has been exorcised. Similarly a person who *already believes* that his present-life problem has a past-life cause may well be susceptible only to that superconscious therapy which capitalizes on his pre-existing delusion.

Few will dispute that no matter how weird or "far out" a neurotic's behaviour, exorcism is most unlikely to cure him if he has no belief in possession. Even fewer will fail to see that, while inducing a possession-belief where none exists may conceivably lead to a cure in exceptional cases, it is far more probable that the cure could turn out to be worse than the disease. And even if the cure worked, the patient would be left with a belief that had the capacity to do him harm at a later date.

Past-life therapy could be justified if it was used only on patients who already believed they were victims of traumatic past-life experiences. Unfortunately, past-life therapists actually induce such beliefs in patients who did not previously have them. A past-life therapist may claim that he can treat non-believers successfully. But anyone with even a rudimentary understanding of superconscious processes is aware that the mind cannot induce any behaviour modification based on a premise that it does not believe. Patients of past-life therapists are in fact induced to believe that their superconscious fantasies are remembrances of events in which they really did participate in a previous incarnation. And that belief can be intolerable.

In a case described by Ian Wilson,[4] whom the hypnotist involved, Wilf Proudfoot, allowed to listen to the unpublished tape recordings, a man named John Pollock was curious about his possible past lives and was superconsciously regressed at his own request. He produced several past lives of an insignificant nature, impossible to investigate, but finally declared that he was a person from history about whom much documentation survived.

Pollock claimed to be Dr. Nehemiah Bradford, a surgeon who had lived in Frenchay, a short distance from Pollock's own home of Bristol, in the late eighteenth and early nineteenth centuries. Pollock had heard of Bradford, and had actually seen Bradford's house, still standing more than a century after Bradford's death. He had not, however, acquired any information about Bradford beyond the facts already stated, and that proved significant.

Pollock, as Bradford, described his successful career as a surgeon and his marriage to one Rachel Brewiss. He was then taken forward to Bradford's old age and asked to describe his circumstances. He declared that his wife had recently died, and he was living in the house alone except for a young servant girl for whom he felt a discomforting lust. Taken further forward he said that he was now completely alone. He was reluctant to say what had happened to the servant girl.

Pressed for details, Pollock/Bradford confessed that his lust for the girl had finally got the better of him. He had raped her and then, to avoid felony prosecution, murdered her. Asked how he had disposed of the body, he answered that he had waited until there was a fresh grave dug in the nearby churchyard, and under the cover of darkness he had buried her above the other body so that the fresh-dug ground would arouse no suspicions. He had informed the neighbors that the girl had gone to work elsewhere, and he had then lived out the remainder of his life without ever getting caught.

The effect on John Pollock when he heard the tape recording and learned the monstrous crime he had committed in a past life, without even the mitigating circumstance of being caught and punished, was devastating. He sat up with Ian Wilson on the occasion of their meeting until 3:00 a.m., chainsmoking and replaying the incriminating tapes over and over. Because of his strict Catholic upbringing and his belief in reincarnation, his guilt was intolerable. I do not think I am overdramatizing when I suggest that his unbearable guilt may easily have driven him to suicide.

That did not happen, and it seems to me that only his discovery that his superconscious fantasy was *not* a memory of a genuine past life prevented it from happening. For while Dr. Nehemiah Bradford was indeed a person from history, documentation survives that proves beyond any doubt that the rape-murder described by Pollock could not have happened and did not happen.

County records show that the real Dr. Nehemiah Bradford was born in 1749. On the 18th of January 1786 he married, not any Rachel Brewiss but Susannah Rogers, a rich lady. Bradford did not spend his last years in the house Pollock had once seen and in which his superconscious fantasy was set, but in the smaller manor cottage to which he moved on retirement. And he could not have moved in a servant girl to keep house after his wife died, for the very good reason that his wife outlived him! Nehemiah Bradford died December 31st, 1835, at the age of eighty-seven. Susannah Bradford did not die until September 12th, 1837, when she was sixty-nine.

Pollock got right only the details he had learned in his childhood. The rest of his fantasy seems to have been based on a massive gravestone that he had seen at Frenchay's Unitarian Chapel, believed to have been placed there to deter graverobbers; and the story of Dr. Thomas Mountjoy, an eighteenth-century surgeon who murdered a black servant in order to dissect her body.

THE SUPERCONSCIOUS WORLD

Do I really need to stress the disastrous consequences that might have ensued if Pollock had been hypnotized by a 'past-life therapist?' Such a person could not have failed to reinforce Pollock's belief that his fantasized rape-murder had really happened. At best past-life therapy is based on the assumption that reincarnation is an established fact; and reincarnation is *not* an established fact. At worst it is an outrageous fraud that perpetuates superstition and has the potential to do *all* patients the enormous harm it would certainly have done to John Pollock if he had had the misfortune to submit to such quackery. As for the harm that already has been done by past-life quacks: I would have to be very naive to expect to find any such cases in the published accounts of their so-called successes.

There is also a strong risk that a person participating in this type of experiment could be setting himself up for a unique kind of shakedown, as is evidenced by a recent case in Canada. A flamboyant, well-known millionaire entrepreneur was sued by a self-styled psychic who also practised reincarnation therapy, on the grounds that he had consulted her professionally, had based business decisions on her psychic prophecies, and therefore owed her a percentage of the profits he had made since the consultation. A man with less integrity might have allowed himself to be blackmailed into an out-of-court settlement, rather than allow his credulity in consulting her to be held up to public scrutiny.

This case, however, came to court. The judge recognized that the "psychic power" on which the plaintiff based her case does not exist, and ruled in favor of the defendant. The correctness of that verdict is surely confirmed by the fact that allegedly psychic information came from the defendant's own imagination during a superconscious past-life fantasy — a fantasy in which he imagined himself to be a historical person who was still alive at the time of his birth!

I cannot help wondering how that same case might have come out had it been tried in a US court before a district judge up for re-election. I recall a wonderful movie called *Miracle on 34th Street*, in which an elected judge was terrified of having to rule that there is no Santa Claus. Imagine a nationally-known psychic launching a similar suit in a home town where her pretence that she had prophesied a political assassination had made her a local hero. Would the home town judge dare rule against her? The thought frightens me. And even in the Canadian case, where the defendant won, the case still cost him a considerable sum in lawyers' fees, besides causing him immeasurable professional embarrassment.

Past-life therapy is an aberration that, like psychoanalysis in Beverly Hills, is likely to be fashionable for a while and then decline into well-deserved oblivion. Of greater durability is the false notion that a superconscious subject must always tell the truth.

It is a fact that information consciously forgotten can remain dormant in the memory and be retrieved under superconsciousness. The man who recalled a passage of Oscan that he had glanced at once and not consciously remembered, is perhaps the best example. In my concerts I often regress subjects to their tenth and fourth birthdays and ask them such questions as: "What are you wearing?" "What presents did you receive?" "What did you have for breakfast this morning?" "Who sits next to you at school?" "What is your teacher's name?" The subject invariably gives an answer, and those answers fall into three categories:

    a) true answers, where the information has remained in the conscious memory
    b) true answers, where the information has not been consciously remembered but has remained dormant and been retrieved by superconscious memory enhancement
    c) fantasized answers that do *not* accord with the facts of the subject's past.

There is *no way* of knowing into which of those three categories any particular answer falls, except where the accuracy of the answer can be independently verified. While it may be true that all information ever acquired survives somewhere in the recesses of the dormant memory, it is not true that consciously forgotten information can always be accurately recalled under superconsciousness.

The unreliability of information elicited by superconscious techniques was graphically demonstrated in an experiment conducted by Dr. David Marks of Otago University in New Zealand in 1984 for a television documentary on hypnotism. Dr. Marks obtained the cooperation of three secretaries from the television station who proved susceptible to deep superconscious suggestion. After a few preliminary experiments at the TV station offices, he invited all three to lunch, giving them no hint that the main experiment was still in progress. As the four pulled to a stop in front of the restaurant and alighted from his car, an "armed robbery" was committed by three people at the service station directly across the road from where they were parked. The three secretaries had a clear view of the entire proceedings. They saw the thieves complete the rather noisy robbery and get away in a car.

In front of the police and executives from the TV studio, Marks reintroduced each of the three subjects separately into the superconscious state. All three gave a most detailed description of the crime, including the number of perpetrators, the make and color of the car, and other relevant details. None of the three agreed with either of the others. The color of the car varied in the three accounts, as did the number and sex of the robbers. Each retelling brought out fresh contradictions, and none of the secretaries' accounts was close to the actual facts of the event.

As you might have guessed by now, the robbery was a simulation, conducted for the sole purpose of measuring the accuracy of superconscious memory enhancement. The comparison of the true event with the three widely different hypnotized witnesses' accounts destroyed once and for all the conceit that testimony given under hypnosis is as reliable as a photograph. The danger of presenting such testimony to a jury conditioned to believe that a hypnotized person cannot lie is self-evident.

Marks' experiment proved what experienced operators have known for a long time. I have been saying the same thing on radio, television, and newspaper interviews since 1961. I am always willing to induce the superconscious state in a witness in the hope that he will recall details that could lead the police to the perpetrators of a crime; but I never fail to point out that any information thus elicited must be independently verified, as there can be no guarantee that it will be correct. Nonetheless, many police forces in North America are now hiring hypnotists, or alternatively requiring some officers to take courses in hypnotism, in the belief that hypnotism is the new "magic bullet" to replace the discredited lie detector.

THE SUPERCONSCIOUS WORLD

I must emphasize this point: as an investigative tool, superconscious memory enhancement can be useful to an operator who realizes that information thus elicited may or may not be true; but it is not a truth serum. In the hands of a misinformed operator — or even worse, an unscrupulous one — it can be used to pervert justice. For example, an investigator who wants a witness to identify a particular suspect is likely, consciously or unconsciously, to convey his wishes to the subject. In such a case it is by no means improbable that the subject will fantasize the appropriate recollection for the purpose of pleasing the operator. The false evidence thus implanted into a susceptible memory could then be reproduced later, even in court, in a most convincing way, with the subject absolutely convinced that he was telling the truth.

The question arises at this point: Why would the watchdog allow such a thing to happen? The answer is that the subject, at all levels of awareness, implicitly believes that a police officer who *knows* who committed a crime must be right. Fantasizing a memory that corroborates what the police think they already *know*, therefore helps the cause of law and order. For that reason it is imperative that all such sessions be conducted in the presence of competent witnesses and recorded, and that testimony elicited be treated as the equivalent of a hunch.

Unfortunately that seldom happens. Lawmen who practise this line of investigation tend to take themselves too seriously. Some have even formed a professional society to which they have given the rather lofty title, Forensic Hypnotists' Association (amongst other similar titles). Fortunately the courts are rectifying the situation by ruling hypnotically-enhanced memories/fantasies inadmissable.

I earlier mentioned Coué's discovery that all effective superconscious suggestion is auto-suggestion. Superconsciousness that is totally self-induced is far more a fact of everyday life than most people realize.

Two thousand years ago, as mentioned earlier, many persons formed the delusion that they were possessed. Although it was their cultural environment that conditioned them into the belief that possession was possible, no external suggestion ever convinced any individual that *he* was possessed. That conviction had to come from within himself. And every time the victim of such a delusion evinced possession symptoms, by his own behaviour he reinforced his delusion and intensified the auto-suggestion. A clearer instance of self-hypnosis would be hard to find.

Possession disappeared and was replaced by witchcraft. Now witchcraft has been replaced by the superconscious play-acting known as multiple personality. The popularity of *The Three Faces of Eve* created an environment in which copycat cases became an epidemic. But as with possession, no individual evinced multiple-personality symptoms as a result of external suggestion. The suggestion that fantasized alternative personalities were real had to come from within himself.

Far more pernicious than multiple-personality delusion, which enriches only a few best-selling authors and costs the average believer no more than the price of a book, is the latest spiritualism/reincarnation/possession scam known as "channeling." Until it was touted in a 1985 autobiographical fantasy novel (labelled non-fiction!) written by a very famous and very gullible actress and later made into a television mini-series, the new spiritualism was no more successful in fleecing the public than modern astrology or tea leaf reading. Since then, thanks to endorsement by the rich and ignorant, the medium promoted in the book has succeeded in parting large numbers of marks from large sums of money. For example, in a single weekend seminar, allegedly presided over by a 35,000 year old American Indian spirit guide, she separated 700 believers from $400 each, for a total of $280,000.

The medium was J.Z. Knight, a housewife from Tacoma, Washington. Anyone who was favorably impressed by the carefully-rehearsed nonsense of the mini-series is urged to watch for a rerun of the ABC television program "20/20," in which Knight was featured. According to magazine editor Robert Basil, the very language used by Knight's alleged 35,000-year-old spirit guide from the mythical land of Atlantis (how did he learn English?) exposed Knight as "clearly a charlatan, a psychotic, or some of both." [5]

According to *Time*, channeling involves "a variety of techniques that may include meditation, yoga, hypnosis and fealty to a guru." [6] The *Newsweek* account quotes Carl Raschke, professor of religious studies at the University of Denver, as believing that the medium "puts herself in a powerful self-induced hypnotic state that mesmerizes an audience." [7]

THE SUPERCONSCIOUS WORLD

The medium, it seems, is as much a victim of auto-induced self-delusion as her followers. I wonder if I gave *myself* the superconscious suggestion that I was possessed by a million-year-old Missing Link, and started spouting stereotyped Hollywood Indian, could I make $280,000 in a weekend? It is an interesting thought. And several years after I coined the word superconscious to describe a person in the state of heightened suggestibility discovered by Anton Mesmer, the spook gurus are now using that same word to mean something equivalent to possessed.

Channeling may well be the ultimate scam. For, whereas the old style spook-crooks used conjuring tricks performed in darkened rooms by hidden assistants, tricks that a competent investigator such as Houdini could detect and expose, the new fraud relies on the "big lie" technique of offering only unsubstantial claims that can be neither proven nor disproven. This take-my-word-for-it approach to the bunco racket deprives them of all but the most gullible and undiscriminating marks. But, as Rasputin amply demonstrated, one rich and powerful sucker can be better than a thousand poor ones.

Spiritualism is not the only old con that is new again. India's fakirs have long encouraged the belief that they can float in the air in defiance of gravity. Recently, the Maharishi Mahishi Yogi has started charging selected marks enormous fees for teaching them to levitate. In fact, they are taught to bounce up and down on a mattress until either they recognize that they have been hoaxed and depart, or a self-induced superconscious time-dilation fantasy causes them to imagine that a great length of time is passing during the fraction of a second that they are in the air.

Another kind of self-induced superconscious delusion was chronicled in the British national newspapers, September 16-20, 1980.[8] A thirty-nine-year-old man was charged with participating in a sexual relationship, over a nine-month period, with a fourteen-year-old girl, at a time when the age of consent was sixteen years. The main testimony against the accused was the girl's diary, which she vehemently maintained was true in every detail. The diary recounted sexual encounters between the man and the girl at his office, in his car, in a sauna, and in various properties to which his position as a real-estate agent gave him access.

THE SUPERCONSCIOUS WORLD

The girl's diary was fiction, as was her whole story. The man was able to provide unimpeachable alibis for several of the times that he was alleged to have been with his accuser. And some of the more graphic passages in the girl's diary were shown to have been borrowed from two novels by Harold Robbins.

What makes this case relevant is that the girl was not consciously lying. Because she so desperately *wanted* her erotic fantasies to be true, she had succeeded in giving herself the superconscious suggestion that they *were* true. Psychiatrist Dr. Steven Shaw explains:[9]

> In some individuals the dividing line between fantasy and reality becomes very blurred. And examples *par excellence* are immature children, particularly girls. Added to this is that at fourteen they are sexually restrained — they are guarded more harshly by their parents than are boys. And that means that their fantasies can become more enmeshed and develop until they spill over and become such a part of their lives that they assume a "reality."

No one can criticize laws that protect our children from molestation by adults. But the above case and many others like it show the need for thorough investigation of such allegations before charges are laid and reputations destroyed.[10] And while the girl in the British case was never questioned under hypnosis, it is my professional opinion that, had she been, she would have continued to maintain her fantasy.

Persons who use superconscious fantasies to feed their egos are not rare. Proponents of ESP, UFOs, astrology, palmistry, phrenology, Velikovskyan physics, psychic archaeology, Von Daniken's space gods, and assorted medical quackeries, have proven impervious to the most conclusive evidence that their beliefs are false. Any belief formed and maintained by conscious reasoning can be discarded if evidence is forthcoming that proves the falseness of such a belief. A belief that has been auto-reinforced in the superconscious, usually because it is emotionally comforting, cannot be shaken by any amount of contrary evidence. Believers in all of the above-mentioned unrealities are, to use an archaic term, self-hypnotized.

High on the ladder of self-deception are the self-styled psychics. Psychics come in two kinds: those who actually believe that they have some kind of paranormal power; and those who pretend to believe that they have such power. The former are sincere but self-deluded; the latter are humbugs. The former see their one percent of fulfilled lucky guesses as proof that they are special, and remove the ninety-nine percent of unfulfilled guesses from their conscious memory as quickly as possible. The latter deliberately make a hundred wild guesses with a ten-percent probability of fulfillment, confident that *National Inquirer* will headline the ten "hits" and suppress the ninety misses.

While the sincere-but-deluded group is by far the larger, few if any of its members seek fame. The humbug group includes such luminaries as Uri Geller, Peter Hurkos, Kreskin, and Jeane Dixon, each of whom has been discredited or shown to be fraudulent so many times that by their very continuance they show themselves to be conscious hoaxers.

Thanks to the continuing media fiction, many people believe that psychics have often aided law-enforcement agencies in solving crimes. This is simply not true. While some investigators have indeed become sufficiently frustrated or gullible to allow a psychic to interfere in an investigation, there has not been one single instance of a psychic providing any useful information. On the occasion that Peter Hurkos informed the news media that he was helping the FBI in a nationally publicized case, the Bureau had him arrested for impersonating a Federal officer. As for Jeane Dixon's famous prophesying of the assassination of American President John F. Kennedy, she did indeed make such a prophecy — after the event.

Uri Geller once told an interviewer, "Magicians can do everything I do — but they have to use trickery." That was true as far as it went. What Geller omitted to mention was that *he* is a magician.[11] His failure to make an adequate living as a legitimate magician caused him to start preying on the gullible, a category that includes an alarming number of psychologists and scientists, competent in other areas but totally unable or unwilling to detect subterfuge when testing so-called psychics. It is interesting to note that Geller's powers fail to materialize whenever an investigative magician, including "Tonight Show" host Johnny Carson, sets up conditions that make trickery impossible.

THE SUPERCONSCIOUS WORLD

Kreskin at times comes close to being an honest magician, but his pretence that he utilizes abilities other than conjuring skills is reprehensible. Dr. David Marks and Dr. Richard Kammann have written an enlightening book titled *The Psychology of the Psychic*,[12] that deals with the claims and performances of Kreskin and Geller, as well as examining the incredible gullibility of the "serious" parapsychologists who have pronounced their conjuring tricks genuinely paranormal.

Despite my impatience with parapsychologists who, in the face of overwhelming evidence, refuse to recognize that they have been deceived by magicians' tricks, I have never been tempted to prove that they *are* gullible by deceiving them myself. James Randi has done that very thoroughly.

Randi's "Project Alpha" is worth describing in some detail.[13] For years Randi and other members of the Committee for the Scientific Investigation of Claims of the Paranormal had been telling parapsychologists that they were being deceived by conjurers. Committee members had many times offered to set up test conditions under which trickery would be impossible, so that any positive results could genuinely be attributed to factors other than deliberate deceit. The parapsychologists' uncompromising refusal to admit that they could be deceived, and their stubborn conceit that they could not fail to detect any experimental subject who achieved positive results in ESP tests by cheating, left Randi with no alternative but to demonstrate graphically that they were wrong.

Two teenage magicians, coached by Randi, successfully infiltrated the parapsychology department of Washington University in St. Louis by posing as psychics. For the next two years the magicians preyed on the parapsychologists' gullibility, faking test after test and causing the parapsychologists jubilantly to proclaim that here at last was the "clear proof, impossible to fake," that ESP demonstrably and beyond question did exist. Even when Randi himself hinted to the experimenters that perhaps they were again being duped by conjuring, they still refused to believe that he might be right.

After two years, Randi called a press conference at which he and his two teenage confederates finally exposed the hoax. The parapsychologists, instead of acknowledging that they *were* easily deceived, and incorporating the safeguards proposed by magicians into their research, screamed "dirty pool" — and continued to obtain positive results by maintaining test conditions that did not rule out cheating! Some even continued to argue that they could not be deceived and had not been deceived, and that the magicians who deceived them really *were* psychics who for some reason were now pretending to have used conjuring techniques. As Barnum may or may not have said: There's a sucker born every minute. Some of those suckers, unfortunately, have PhDs.

I am forced to conclude that there is no such thing as a psychic. Hundreds of thousands of man-hours of *competent* investigation of the claims of alleged psychics has failed to turn up anything but conscious fraud (e.g., Uri Geller) and self-delusion (e.g., Edgar Cayce). Certainly *I* am not a psychic, and have never claimed to be. Rather I have stated in every interview and on stage before millions of people over the years, and I repeat here, that I have no psychic or extra-sensory powers, and in all my years of touring the world I have never met anyone who does have such powers. Yet despite this admission, I continue to run into persons who insist that I do have psychic powers and am for some reason refusing to acknowledge them. Such people are beyond the reach of evidence, logic or reason. They have emotionally satisfying beliefs, and such beliefs, once auto-reinforced in the superconscious, can survive an infinite amount of falsification.[14]

Consider those people who believe that they have valid premonitions. In fact we have all had premonitions, expectations of specific effects that we have no conscious reason to expect, since we are not aware of possessing any information that would justify such expectations. Most of the time such premonitions are random thoughts that pop into our heads in the absence of any triggering stimulus, and they are fulfilled no more often than statistical probability would dictate.

There is, however, another kind of premonition, based on information not known to the conscious memory but known to the superconscious. Although not obtained by psychic or extra-sensory means, it may have been obtained subliminally without any conscious realization of the fact (like the passage of Oscan). It is reasonable to conclude that the human mind does not have extra-sensory capacities, since hundreds of thousands of man-hours over more than a century have failed to find any. But the mind does have innate capacities beyond anything that has ever been charted or identified.

The most clearly attested but not-understood power of the human mind is its capacity for superconscious reasoning. We have all heard of people who, stumped by a difficult problem, "sleep on it" and wake up with the solution. And we have seen mystery movies in which the super-cop, utilizing only information that was also available and subliminally known to the audience, suddenly brings it all together and knows "whodunnit." When something like this happens, and a problem is solved at the superconscious level while the conscious mind is focussed elsewhere, we have what psychologists call the "aha! syndrome." The best-known historical example of the aha! syndrome was the revelation that caused Archimedes to spring from his bath and run naked through the streets shouting, "Eureka!"

Superconscious reasoning does not, however, always produce an "aha!" Sometimes an answer is deduced to a question that conscious thinking has never formulated. As that answer begins to seep into the mind's consciousness, the effect is not an "aha!" but a premonition. And where a future event may have a probability of two percent based on information consciously acknowledged, once the superconscious processes have incorporated information not consciously recognized as relevant, that probability might rise to sixty percent or higher. When a premonition's probability of fulfillment is as high as sixty percent, subsequent fulfillment is rather less supernatural or paranormal than believers in the occult like to imagine.

Anyone can have a superconscious premonition. When two or three such premonitions are followed by fulfillment, and the individual concerned fails to recognize that they were based on information known to him subliminally, cultural acceptance of the psychic concept may cause him to believe that he is psychic. Once that belief is imprinted and then reinforced in the superconscious, it is invariably there to stay. And psychics often do immeasurable harm to persons who believe in and act upon their capricious advice.

The question now arises: if the watchdog can be subverted to a completely unreal standard of values by cultural conditioning, why should it not be similarly manipulated by a hypnotist? The answer lies in the clear distinction between auto- (self) and hetero- (external) suggestion. Under no circumstances can the watchdog be persuaded to accept a new set of values dictated by an external source. Before the watchdog, or conscience, can be persuaded to change its position one iota, it must be programmed from within. To put it another way, the watchdog is at all times fully aware of external reality; but external reality is whatever the conscious mind perceives it to be. Cultural conditioning can manipulate conscious beliefs, and those conscious beliefs in turn program the watchdog.

Mutually contradictory beliefs create a condition called cognitive dissonance, that exists when the conscious mind recognizes that it is acting inconsistently. An obvious example is that of a person who knows that smoking causes cancer and several other crippling diseases that kill thousands of human beings every year, but who nonetheless continues to smoke or encourages others to do so. When the mind recognizes that a contradiction exists, it eliminates the inconsistency by whatever means is necessary. In the case of the smoker the obvious solution would be to quit smoking. But if, through habit, that proves impossible, the mind resolves the conflict by the only other means available: by superconsciously ridding itself of the belief that smoking is harmful!

In the case of the person whose job it is to promote the sale of tobacco products, the first solution to the semi-conscious realization that he is an accessory and co-conspirator to mass homicide, is to seek employment elsewhere. As often as not, however, economic realities eliminate that as a practical course of action. The solution here, also, is to stop believing that tobacco is harmful. You have probably seen advertisements, written and signed by tobacco company executives, which declare that doctors who denounce smoking are in effect incompetent ignoramuses. If you have ever wondered whether such promotors of death are conscious slaughterers willing to sacrifice thousands of lives for the almighty dollar, or merely mindless, scientifically illiterate morons incapable of evaluating statistical evidence, the answer is that they are neither.

Promotors of smoking are nothing more than victims of contradictory beliefs who have succeeded in anesthetizing their consciences. They have convinced themselves that, since they are not criminals who would deliberately hurt anyone, and since their economic welfare depends on their ability to promote tobacco sales, smoking *must* be harmless. And

THE SUPERCONSCIOUS WORLD

because that is what they must believe in order to live with themselves, that is what they do believe. George Orwell called their thought processes "doublethink."

We have seen how, under superconsciousness, individuals have relived the witnessing of a crime and given descriptions of the event that did not accord with reality. We have seen individuals relive past lives in which they were involved with people from history, and incorporate into those lives fictitious characters from historical novels dealing with the same period. We should therefore not be surprised that many people, under the subliminal prompting of a hypnotist who believes in flying saucers, have described how they were kidnapped by alien beings, taken aboard a space ship, stripped naked and physically examined. Such people, like subjects who fantasize past lives on demand, are telling the hypnotist what they know or believe he wants to hear. Superconscious obedience fully explains their stories.

I have mentioned the intense desire of a superconscious subject to please the operator. On my own stage when I regress volunteers to "past lives," I carefully avoid giving the impression that I have any doubts as to the reality of reincarnation, for then a sizable number of volunteers would pick up on my disbelief and fail to fantasize at all — and I am in the business of entertaining an audience. Consequently, night after night dozens of volunteers give detailed, entertaining descriptions of imagined lives that are partly enhanced dormant memories from *this* life, and partly pure fantasy. In keeping with my policy of presenting only *honest* entertainment, I make sure after the demonstration that no one leaves my stage believing that any sequence in which he participated was anything more than a superconscious dream.

Perhaps the best known weavers of "I was kidnapped by flying sorcerers" tales were Barney Hill and his wife. The Hills were not childish morons as many people imagined, telling a modern fairy tale that only a six-year-old could expect to be believed. Rather, Barney was hypnotized by a man whom he knew to be a member of a UFO "research" cult, and he obediently fantasized an abduction by the occupants of a flying saucer because he recognized that that was what the hypnotist wanted to hear. When Mrs. Hill was hypnotized later, she had already heard Barney's fantasy and she obediently corroborated it.

THE SUPERCONSCIOUS WORLD

People who believe that the superconscious, or hypnotism, or astral awareness, or cosmic consciousness, or mediumistic trance, or any of the other names that have been given to overt and subliminal suggestion, is a hot line to the Absolute, are as deluded as those persons who dogmatically assert that the superconscious state does not exist.

Up to this point I have been stressing the limitations of superconscious suggestion, spelling out what it cannot do. Obviously I do not have a negative attitude toward my own specialty. Rather, I felt it necessary to dispose of the ridiculous before proceeding to the sublime.

The theory of superconscious suggestion has not advanced greatly since Braid and Coué. But that does not mean that all progress has ceased. In the past three decades in particular, there have been many men and women who have brought the science of applied suggestion, particularly in the field of medicine, to the forefront of twentieth-century thinking.

The best of the post-Second-World-War British medical hypnotists is without a doubt Dr. Philip Magonet of Harley Street, London. Dr. S.J. Van Pelt would of course disagree, since he was somewhat of a strutting peacock who believed himself to be the rightful holder of that title. Van Pelt's writings and findings are of unquestioned importance, but he was something of a publicity seeker, whereas Magonet was content to win the respect of his peers within the medical profession. Magonet's published papers on the treatment of asthma would have been sufficient by themselves to guarantee his place in medical history, but even more important were his papers on the application of superconscious suggestion in a host of other medical situations. In my view those papers should be required reading for any doctor contemplating the use of superconscious therapy in his practice.[15]

In America, one of the pioneers of medical hypnosis in general practice was Dr. Thomas A. Clawson Jr of Salt Lake City, Utah. Clawson's belief in the potential of suggestion in medicine led him to defy the initial opposition of his Church and persevere until the hierarchy were satisfied that superconscious techniques constituted a legitimate adjunct to medical practice and officially accepted them as such. His writings were published in medical journals throughout the USA. In particular, his technique for treating the smoking habit was one of the best I have yet encountered.

THE SUPERCONSCIOUS WORLD

Tom Clawson's belief in his life's work, his family and his Church was total and never wavered. I many times urged him to write a book on his thousands of cases so that future generations could benefit from his knowledge. He never did. When he was terminally ill with cancer, he used his own techniques to control pain and dispense with any chemical assistance. He was my friend, and I miss him.

On the use of superconscious suggestion in obstetrics, everything a practitioner needs to know can be found in the works of Dr. William Kroger.[16] I disagree with Kroger on one minor point. He suggests that the time to start using suggestion with a patient is in the sixth month of pregnancy. In my own experience, working in conjunction with obstetricians with my wife as patient, I found that the early use of superconscious suggestion was effective in preventing morning sickness, and that it made the entire experience a breeze.

The man who has probably contributed most to the recent advancement of superconscious suggestion techniques in medicine is psychiatrist Dr. Milton Erickson. Dr. Erickson's books are filled with accounts of patients whose crippling habits and dysfunctions he cured. It is true that some of Dr. Erickson's published accounts of his cases involve hard-to-believe coincidences and improbabilities, but the cases are so thoroughly documented that suspicion of exaggeration is dispelled.

Erickson's *ad hoc* suggestion-treatments are in every case replicable and testable, and my own experience causes me to believe that they would work. He had an almost uncanny instinct for the right approach to a specific patient or problem, and the fully-detailed techniques described in his abundance of publications should constitute the standard procedures for a whole generation of suggestion therapists.

Medical hypnotist Dr. Bernard Stern of New York, whose excellent work in that city has deservedly brought him respect and esteem, in 1978 sent me a new book by Doctors Herbert and David Spiegel.[17] The Spiegels are a brilliant father and son team who have achieved justified recognition in the eastern United States, and their book demonstrates why. It is a most informative volume. I do not endorse a technique they describe, in which a patient is asked to fill out a form called a Hypnotic Induction

Profile Scoresheet, but I recognize that by its very use it could have the effect of causing the patient to become more suggestible.

A man I long admired professionally, and whom I knew as a friend, was Professor Fred T. Kolough of the department of psychiatry, University of Utah College of Medicine. Being a skilled surgeon as well as a medical hypnotist, he has by his knowledge and insight into the use of suggestion in the convalescence of surgical patients, expanded the use of suggestion-therapy as an important support system in modern medical practice. His death in 1986 created a void that will be hard to fill.

All of the persons acknowledged above, as well as hundreds of other dedicated researchers, have advanced the use of suggestion in the therapeutic field, and this can only give one a sanguine feeling for the future. Unfortunately, the bed of roses does have its thorns.

I recently heard an alleged psychologist in Los Angeles inform a talk-show host that he specializes in convincing women under hypnosis that their recently-divorced spouses never existed. I can think of many arguments against the use of such therapy, not the least of which is that those who forget the lessons of history are bound to repeat its mistakes. I can think of no valid benefits of such a technique.

Similarly, in 1964 I met a prison psychiatrist from Washington state who boasted that he had one prisoner so susceptible to suggestion that he had only to clap his hands and the unfortunate subject would drop his bucket and fall over in front of the other prisoners. I can't picture other inmates lining up all night to receive that kind of therapy.

Controlled suggestion has come of age. It will never have the role in medicine that Anton Mesmer and his successors imagined, since it is not a substitute for surgery, antibiotics or even, except in rare cases, chemical anesthesia. But as an adjunct to a physician's other resources and procedures its value is no longer in dispute. As for the use of superconscious suggestion in entertainment, I feel justified in declaring that my concerts are as far removed from the carnival demonstrations in which subjects were made to eat candles and soap, as modern medicine is removed from bloodletting and exorcisms.

CHAPTER SEVEN

A SUPERCONSCIOUS TRAVELER'S TALES

It was always my ambition to be part of the world of the theater, and Australia was in many ways a great country for a young boy with such ambitions to grow up in. Vaudeville was alive and well at the Tivoli Theater in Melbourne, and would remain so even beyond the advent of television in 1956. Impressionable eyes and ears could take in the acts of the finest performers that England, Europe and America had to offer. The entire drama class of my high school was taken to see the Oliviers starring in the Old Vic Company's production of *Richard III*. Drama clubs and small suburban theater societies were in abundance for those bitten by the "arts" bug. It may well be that this book would have been written by an actor in mid-career, except for one of those strange strokes of fate that sometimes dictate one's destiny.

I was roughly six months into my thirteenth year when I happened to read a newspaper article concerning a military chaplain who had entertained some Australian soldiers in New Guinea during the war by hypnotizing six members of their platoon. The article included an explanation of his methodology for achieving this. I tried it on a school friend and it worked. Knowing nothing of the reasons behind that amazing result, I left well enough alone in the practical sense and began to haunt second-hand book stores in order to pick up and read everything I could find on the subject. Many of the books I discovered were the same research texts from which I have quoted in earlier chapters.

THE SUPERCONSCIOUS WORLD

Out of curiosity grew a respect for the status of hypnotism as a basic science of suggestion and not some psychically-produced power. I had no thought in mind for it ever to become an important part of my life's work. My mind, you see, was made up. I was going to be an actor. I would apply for a scholarship to attend the Royal Academy of Dramatic Arts in London.

Shortly after finishing high school, and while waiting to be called for the scholarship auditions, I attended a party consisting mostly of older adults. As a point of discussion, I brought up the subject of hypnotism. I was immediately attacked (verbally) by my elders for dabbling in dangerous witchcraft. Logical rebuttals of their arguments proved impossible, for their minds were frozen to further explanation. I confess I left in somewhat of a huff.

On the way home that night the germ of an idea began. What, I wondered, would be the result if I were to combine traditional theater with the science of hypnotism? Could I thereby present a concert that would both instruct and entertain? I thought this through for the next few weeks, and slowly but surely put together a script that I felt would fill the bill on both accounts.

I chose for my initial try-out a spot on the bill of a variety show being presented for charity. The performers were a group known as the Sunshine Concert Party, and I was assigned a place in the second half. I had previously done several ten-minute spots with the group, in between acting in regional plays, in order to keep my hand in as a conjurer. This time, however, I asked the producer if I could do thirty minutes, and he somewhat reluctantly agreed. I invited many of the detractors from the house party, since they had been, in effect, the catalyst for this experiment.

The audience response to my performance surpassed anything I had remotely expected. I had over fifty volunteers, and twenty-one of them were successful subjects for the demonstration. The applause at the end was enthusiastic and gratifying. The previous detractors told me afterwards that I had been right, and that I should continue to present concerts whenever and wherever possible.

THE SUPERCONSCIOUS WORLD

Unfortunately, the audience's enthusiasm was not shared by the show's producer. After making some speculative remarks about my parentage, he informed me that I had been on stage for eighty-two minutes and had ruined the remainder of the concert. He suggested, with his colorful vocabulary, that I should in future take my talents elsewhere. It was sound advice. I said goodbye to acting, and embarked on the career that would take me to the largest part of the English-speaking world over the next thirty years.

That initial performance was not, however, the beginning of an unbroken run of successes. It was followed by my first attempt at a one-man show, and the results of that . . . . Let me tell you about it.

I had posters and handbills printed without photos of myself, as I felt that I looked too young to be convincing. As both producer and performer, I rented a hall in the Melbourne suburb of Plenty, and purchased an optimistically-large cashbox for holding the rolls of tickets and the money. When our small crew arrived at the hall, we found a group of six local citizens already lined up out front. It was an auspicious beginning. But wait!

We found that we had left the key to the cashbox at home. No matter — the show must go on. The future repository of the box office receipts was unceremoniously smashed against the door frame until it broke open. We were ready to admit our waiting customers. What we were not ready for was the discovery that all six were there only because they had received free tickets for displaying posters in their store windows. The total take on that memorable night was not sufficient to cover the cost of the smashed cashbox, let alone pay the hall rent.

Then there was Hurstbridge. Whenever I start to feel like a "big shot," stepping on stage night after night to sold-out audiences of twenty-eight hundred people, I remember Hurstbridge and it helps balance my perspective.

My worthy manager at the time made an arrangement with the owner of a Hurstbridge milk bar. Seventy-five chairs for customers were placed at one end of the establishment's dining area, leaving room for a stage at the other end. I would describe Hurstbridge (at the time) as a hamlet, except that it was not that big. But my manager had secured excellent terms. I was to keep all proceeds from ticket sales, paying no rent. The owner expected to make his money selling milk shakes, soft drinks and candies during the intermission. I would, of course, provide six free seats for his family.

At about 7:15 p.m. a small crowd began to gather in front of the milk bar. My manager, resplendent in a new powder blue tuxedo, informed me that a big star from the City should not be seen by his public before a show, and that I should therefore retreat to my dressing room and change into my stage attire. I did so, and from the dressing room, which on non-performance days served as a public toilet, I heard Management proudly announce that the box office was open for business.

At 7:30 p.m. my manager breathlessly rushed back to tell me that the crowd now numbered more than twenty, and he could feel the sensation of crisp new pound notes about to be paid into our hands. He returned and made a further announcement about the immediate availability of tickets.

Then came 7:40 p.m. My ashen-faced manager slunk to my dressing room and, through the door (perhaps he feared that I would throttle him?), gave me the news that the "picture bus" had pulled up and the entire crowd had clambered aboard to go to the Panton Hills movie theater two miles away. I was left with, as you no doubt guessed, the shop owner and five members of his family.

Fortunately, not all of my early shows met with the same dearth of customers. Most of them in fact drew audiences ranging from 100 to 200 people. It is hard to believe I once regarded 200 people in the audience as the height of success, when today I often have 300 or more volunteers streaming on to the stage from audiences numbering over 2000. But entertainers have to pay their dues, and I was no exception.

It was soon after Hurstbridge that an enterpreneur named Harry Rooklyn, brother of the internationally-known illusionist Maurice Rooklyn, introduced me to show business promoter Bob Parker. Bob had derived a good deal of fame the previous year by managing the tour of magician

THE SUPERCONSCIOUS WORLD

John Carson, whose specialty was catching bullets in his teeth. "What do you do?" Bob asked. I explained that I could hypnotize, give memory demonstrations and perform feats of conjuring. He squinted his eyes and said, "Fine, but you need a 'Hot Point,' something that will draw the crowds into the tent to see it."

I asked Maurice Rooklyn for advice and he offered to sell me his spectacular illusion, Cheating the Gallows, in which a person is hanged, disappears in mid-air, and reappears instantly at the back of the theater — or in our case, tent. Parker approved, and he had banners painted depicting this death-defying feat. My assistant at the time was a young lady named Robin. Parker felt that the act would draw best if we were billed as a brother-sister act. We became The Amazing Reveens, and Robin was styled "The Girl They Cannot Hang." Parker's tent seated about 100 people, and the stage and gallows were erected at one end.

The Australian fairground was the strongest possible test of an entertainer's mettle. A performer who could hold a crowd's attention there could expect to succeed anywhere in the world. In those days each show had to compete for crowds with anywhere from thirty to fifty other midway attractions. Parker dressed me in full-dress tails and put Robin in a fancy cocktail dress. Doubling as his own barker, he challenged the crowd to match my amazing memory, and then invited volunteers to come into the tent and be hypnotized.

Parker told the story of John Lee, a man who had cheated the gallows in England. He went on to explain that Robin was a contortionist who had trained her body to defy the drop from the gallows. Tying a hangman's noose, he dramatically informed the curious onlookers of the consequences for her if she did not escape in the fraction of a second after the executioner threw the lever. He ended with the announcement that the box office was now open for the next show. The crowds poured in.

The show started with my memorizing the names of thirty objects called out by the audience. Each was assigned a number between one and thirty, and the act concluded with my reciting the entire list backwards and forwards. If anyone wonders how I am able to perform such difficult feats of memory night after night, the answer is practice. After doing an average of ten shows a day on the midway, involving a total of three hundred unrelated articles, with only ten to fifteen minutes rest between shows, my present schedule of one show a night is practically a holiday.

Following the memory act, I did a demonstration of hypnotism that lasted about thirty minutes. The finale was Cheating the Gallows, with Robin vanishing in mid-air and instantly reappearing at the back of the tent crying, "Here I am!" And as if performing was not enough, I also helped rig the tent at the beginning of an engagement, dismantle it afterwards, load and unload the truck, and help drive it to the next town.

Presenting a genuine demonstration of hypnotism on the fairgrounds was almost a missionary program. Showgoers were used to seeing the same stooge, show after show, eat a candle or a bar of soap. Just two years before my performance an old carny named Major Wilson had been exposed as a fraud by *The Truth*, Melbourne's equivalent of *National Enquirer*. *Truth* revealed that its reporter had seen the same "volunteer," dressed as a sailor one day and a soldier the next day, eat a candle at a dozen or more different shows. The Major, however, was not easily put down.

The morning after the *Truth* story appeared, a large crowd gathered in front of the Major's tent to jeer and boo. The Major, feigning outraged innocence, stepped to the front of his platform and waved the newspaper at the crowd. "This filthy newspaper," he declared, "has stated that I, Major Wilson, one of the greatest hypnotists of this century, am a fake. I tell you, if that reporter was here right now I'd hypnotize him and make him eat this paper."

"I'm here, mate, and I'm going to write about you again," a voice cried out from the back of the crowd. A man wearing a hat with the word PRESS stuck in the band pushed his way to the front. "You couldn't hypnotize my cat," the man declared.

"Come inside and I'll make you eat your words," the Major challenged. The two marched into the Major's tent — and so did several dozen paying customers. Once inside, they witnessed the hapless reporter, previously a soldier, previously a sailor, eat a large portion of newspaper. Whether he found it tastier than candle wax, we can only guess.

THE SUPERCONSCIOUS WORLD

It was on the fairgrounds that I learned the value of word-of-mouth advertising. By the second day of each engagement the number of people volunteering to be hypnotized had doubled, and toward the end of the week crowds were lined up to buy tickets before we even opened. The hypnotism had become the show's Hot Point, with the spectacular magical illusion being relegated to second place. Friends and relatives of the volunteers were amazed to see me bringing forward their hitherto unknown talents, and doing so without degrading the volunteers.

It was the popularity of what I had considered a minor part of my performance that led me to stake my future on my potential as a hypnotist. At the end of my one-year contract, and having met my wife-to-be, Coral, I quit the fairgrounds circuit to take on the concert field as a full-time hypnotist. The observations I had made of the thousands of volunteers in the tent shows gave me the format that would eventually make me probably the best-known exponent of concert hypnotism in the English-speaking world.

What made the show a success, I am convinced, is that I enhanced and brought forward my volunteers' own talents. All persons, including those who will not admit it or are even unaware of it, have the talent to address and entertain an audience. I felt that, by using my sense of theater, I could utilize superconscious suggestion to become in effect a high-speed director. I would thus be enabled to bring forward performances each night that would equal those of a director working with trained actors whom he had rehearsed for two or three weeks.

There is a good reason why, after thousands of performances, the show is always fresh for me. Each night is a new challenge, with a new batch of strangers coming forward as volunteers. And if I ever start to get complacent, my manager sneaks up behind me and whispers, "Hurstbridge."

I remember my first professional manager. He was a dear old Shakespearean actor named George Coates. George was one-of-a-kind, a man who loved the theater and looked the part. He invariably dressed in blue business suits with hand-tied bow ties, topped off by a velvet-collared Chesterfield coat and silk scarf. His magnificent bald head with tufts of white hair above the ears was crowned by a finely blocked homburg hat.

George was at his most impressive as my emcee. Audiences would sit entranced as his deep baritone voice extolled the virtues and powers of the man they were about to witness. I often wonder what those audiences thought when, after such a massive build-up, the entertainer who walked forward turned out to be a man barely into his twenties and trying bravely to sprout a beard. However, by the end of the concert the applause was always enthusiastic.

George Coates was a brilliant raconteur. His anecdotes gave me many a chuckle, but the one I remember best is this:

> I remember the days when I was an advance man for Robertson's Theatrical Company. We were about to play in Wanganui, New Zealand. I approached the local innkeeper and said, "Good morning, Sir. My name is George Coates and I am the advance man for Robertson's Theatrical Company. Pray tell me, kind Sir, what are your lowest possible terms for theatricals." And he answered, "Bastards!"

That first touring venture was not financially successful, for I was not yet experienced enough to make word-of-mouth work for me. We were playing to an average of about 180 people in small town halls, and it always seemed that the town was just starting to talk about us as we were preparing to move on. And after about six months the rigors of one-night-stands proved too much for George, who was approaching eighty, and we sadly parted company.

That was when Raymond Alfred Saunders entered the picture. It was Ray who taught me the noble art of showmanship. He had once had a large variety show under canvas, and he knew just about everybody in the business. On learning of the towns that I had left with a good reputation but very little money, he suggested an immediate return to each for at least two nights. And it worked. The show's reputation had built further in my absence, and the crowds at the return visits started to exceed 400

THE SUPERCONSCIOUS WORLD

each night, that being the capacity of the small halls. Ray then had me return for a further one night in each, and all performances sold out prior to the show's arrival. From there he took me into cities with populations in the 20,000 to 30,000 range, playing a week at a time in theaters with 800 or even 1000 seats.

After that, Ray decided that we should go back to all of the Queensland cities where I had played with my tent show. Again he was right, and we were an instant success. We continued returning to sold-out performances until 1960, and in the intervening two-and-a-half decades some of my long-run attendance records in that state have remained unbroken.

However, full success in my native country was to be denied me. To be an Australian entertainer in those days was the kiss of death, as far as the big-time entrepreneurs in Melbourne and Sydney were concerned. Year after year we saw doors slammed in our faces and watched less talented English and American entertainers being paid top money while we had to settle for the crumbs. The time had come to take my chances overseas.

In 1958 while playing the Capital Theater in Perth, I had been approached by an American show promoter whom laws against telling the truth in print prevent me from naming (I will refer to him as T.P.). The promoter had already acquired some notoriety by his unsuccessful attempt to persuade a world champion Australian athlete to turn professional. He had offered the athlete one million American dollars. I had just stepped off stage when I was intercepted in the wings by a five-feet tall, cigar-smoking character who looked like an escapee from a Damon Runyan novel. After the free publicity the Australian television stations had given him on account of his offer to the athlete, I had no trouble recognizing him. "Boy," he rasped, "I didn't get *him*, but I'm going to make *you* the biggest star in the United States."

I had not heard from him in two years. But in mid-1960 he contacted me to announce that my American tour was to commence in Honolulu in January of 1961.

We were elated. Sadly, though, Ray Saunders was unable to leave Australia. At the time no one was able to leave the country without a clearance from the taxation department — and Ray had not filed a tax return in over fifty years. Unwilling to stand in my way, he urged me to go on without him, and I reluctantly agreed. So after finishing Queensland in September of 1960, we flew to New Guinea for a few weeks' working holiday. It was the most rugged tour I have ever done. We travelled from town to town in New Guinea sitting in paratroop jump seats in a DC 3 aircraft, with our raised legs resting on the cargo. As often as not the cargo included live animals. The plane had a low ceiling, and often flew between mountain passes with no more than a couple of wingspans clearance on either side.

On one occasion, in order to get from Lae to Rabaul for our opening performance there, we had to fly via Manus Island and Wewak. That was roughly equivalent to flying from Chicago to Los Angeles via New York and Vancouver. The scenery was breathtaking, but in Wewak the port engine magneto failed during take-off and we were stranded for the night. We did, however, still give a show — not in Rabaul but in Wewak. The local hotel owner sent out a notice announcing the show and had it delivered to every resident of Wewak, each of whom had to sign the notice to prove that the messenger had been there. We drew the entire population of Wewak, all 150, most of whom had not seen a touring show in years. They were a most appreciative audience.

From New Guinea we flew to Fiji, where we played concerts in Suva and the surrounding towns. An Indian fakir was touring the island at the time, using a mixture of eastern mysticism and conjuring tricks to bilk many of the native population of their monthly wages. The authorities asked me if I could do anything to counter his influence. When I learned that his *piece de resistance* was a demonstration in which he stretched out on a bed of nails for ten minutes to prove that he was impervious to pain, I was confident that I could. On three previous occasions in Australia I had placed volunteers on beds of nails for up to two hours without their suffering any pain or injury, for the purpose of proving that anyone in a state of superconscious relaxation could be made to perform such a feat.

I had a local carpenter build me a bed of sharp six-inch nails, and put my wife Coral into a state of superconscious relaxation and placed her on it. Coral was in the Qantas Airlines window in the centre of Suva, while I was in a studio of the local radio station hypnotizing her over the radio. We created a Times Square-sized traffic jam. When I returned to the store where Coral was, I used loud speakers aimed into the street to tell the crowds that I was not supernatural and that any person could be made to do this seemingly impossible feat.

Besides selling a lot of tickets, the demonstration also succeeded in its original purpose. The fakir was ruined. After that we were packed to the roof everywhere we played in Fiji. A reporter named Ron Gray from Vancouver, Canada, was among the many friends we made in Suva, and it was he who suggested that my career might benefit from a Canadian tour.

Then T.P. telephoned from Honolulu. He reported that everything was ready for my big opening, but that transfer problems had held up his funds and I would have to pay for my crew's airfares. I complied. Coral and I and the three children we then had flew to Honolulu during the first week of January.

Our arrival in Honolulu was both exciting and somewhat frightening. We had left behind a steadily-building circuit of profitable cities and towns, and come to the largest country in the English-speaking world, on the basis of one man's assurance; and we had no way of knowing whether the show would be accepted by American audiences. The approach to the airport around Diamond Head was one of the most beautiful and impressive experiences for any traveler. The arrival at the airport was one of the most jarring shocks.

T.P. had told me that my visa and work permit would be waiting for me at Honolulu airport. They weren't. Fortunately the U.S. Immigration officer on duty, instead of putting us on the next flight to Australia as he might have done, told me to report to the Federal Building at ten o'clock the next morning. We then went to the airport foyer to search for T.P., and finally found him peeping from behind a column like a hood in a B-grade movie. He sidled up and whispered that he could not be seen with us, but that a friend would take us to our rooms at the Reef Hotel annex.

THE SUPERCONSCIOUS WORLD

In the hotel room we sat facing T.P., who tried to explain what was going on. Because of his connection with boxing in Hawaii, we learned, it would be to our benefit that he not be visible as the man promoting our performances. He introduced us to the men who would be handling our arrangements, and assured us that we could relax and leave everything to them. Perhaps if I had not been so inexperienced I would have realized at once that we were being taken in by a confidence trickster; but I did not.

Our first show, T.P. explained, was to be at the Petty Officers' Club at Pearl Harbour. That would be followed a few days later by a two-week stand at the Honolulu Civic Centre. He painted a picture of the great plans he had for us in the outer islands, to be followed by our triumphal entry into mainland America via San Francisco and the Bay area.

We hardly slept that night, and after a hurried breakfast I went with T.P.'s man to the Immigration office. The officials there, satisfied that theaters and clubs had been properly booked for my performances, were most cooperative and granted me a sixty-day "special ability and merit" visa.

That night at Pearl Harbour, the show was a great success and I received my first standing ovation in America. Then came a rush of radio and television interviews to promote the Civic Centre opening. T.P.'s press agents had done a fine job, but they kept impressing on me that I should never mention T.P.'s name, even in my sleep.

For over a month newspaper columnists such as Eddie Sherman, and radio personalities Aku-head Papule (Hal Lewis) and Lucky Luck, had been running a teaser campaign asking readers and listeners if they knew the whereabouts of the outstanding Australian entertainer known as Reveen. Between that and the interviews, we had a satisfactory audience for the opening. The press reviews were unanimous in their praise for both the professionalism and the genuineness of the show. We were on our way. Or were we?

After that we wasted a week on Molokai, playing two nights in a high school auditorium that, for lack of publicity, were poorly attended. Then four shows at Hilo on the Big Island were sold out. Finally came

THE SUPERCONSCIOUS WORLD

the crowning achievement of T.P.'s entrepreneurial talents, a one-week engagement at a club called the Lava Pit, the dirtiest, dingiest, scummiest place I have ever worked in my career.

Immediately before me on the bill were two of the most untalented and bored-looking strippers in show business. When they were done, the band stand was cleared of instruments and players to make way for my extravaganza. The stage was simply a pie-shaped wedge in one corner of the room. For reasons of professional discipline rather than artistic fervor, I managed to pull off a show each night, despite the heckling of a drunken tourist who sat ringside each night and called out, "Bring back the flesh acts. We want flesh." Surprisingly, the show made money, even though I had as yet not seen any of it.

Even in 1961 hotels and food for a family of five, plus accommodation for T.P.'s people, cost a small fortune. Each week I went along with paying the bills out of my pocket, accepting T.P.'s assurance that all income would be split up at the end of the Hawaiian tour.

We returned to Oahu to play all of the military bases, and finished with a very successful charity show at Pearl Harbour's Block Arena. That night I approached T.P. about settling my out-of-pocket expenses, including our freight and airfares. I also asked about splitting the profits, my share of which amounted to about $30,000. That is a goodly sum even today, but in 1961 it constituted a small fortune.

"Boy," T.P. said, squeezing my shoulder, "you're an artist. Leave me to worry about such things. In the morning we'll go to the bank, get your money, and then sit down and talk over all the plans your old buddy has for you on the mainland."

However, there was no meeting the next morning. T.P. caught an early morning plane out of Honolulu and left us stranded and penniless in a strange land. We were stuck with both our own hotel bills and his. He had taken us not only for all the money we had managed to save in Australia, but also our share of the entire Hawaiian tour.

We were in a dilemma. Facing an uncertain future, we could either slink back to Australia in defeat, a move that could conceivably be permanent, or carry on to an unknown and untested market. I was ready to quit, but Coral suggested that she and the boys return to Australia until I was established, while I trade in my return ticket on a boat ticket to San Francisco. I did so, and arrived there with barely enough money for a Greyhound bus ticket to Vancouver, where Ron Gray was waiting to help me make a new start in Canada.

The boat trip was miserable, although I did find myself sharing an inside cabin with a rather colorful old character. He told me that he continually took ocean cruises all over the world. I remarked that he must have invested wisely to enjoy such a life. "Not at all," he explained. It seems that he had been a building inspector in New York during the administration of mayor Jimmy Walker, and had made so much money in tax-free bribes that years later he could still cruise anywhere he wished.

I have since learned many things about T.P.. He had been a most active promoter of boxing in the days before Hawaii became the fiftieth state, but since then he had been banned from all connection with the sport on account of alleged dishonest and unethical practices. He had then taken a former star of the Harlem Globetrotters basketball team on a Pacific Ocean tour, directed by a company he had formed for the purpose. It was while touring with the basketball star in Australia that T.P. had made his million-dollar offer to the athlete, and on being turned down had then approached me.

I replayed Perth in 1972, and learned then that it was not any altruistic commitment to amateur sport that had kept the athlete from accepting T.P.'s impressive offer. Rather, neither the athlete's family nor his lawyers had been able to find any evidence that T.P. was capable of raising even $10,000, let alone $1,000,000.

The trip from San Francisco to Vancouver was bleak. It was wet and foggy all the way, and I saw very little of the beautiful scenery for which the area is famous. At Bellingham, Washington, I changed into a business suit to go through Canadian immigration, and held my breath. It was a good move. I was hardly questioned, and was granted a six-month visitor's visa. I arrived in Canada on the 16th of March, 1961, with exactly a nickel in my pocket.

THE SUPERCONSCIOUS WORLD

Ron Gray arranged for me to stay, rent-free, with a publisher friend who had a small cottage on Cultus Lake near Chilliwack, B.C., until we could get some shows going. A lakefront cottage in British Columbia in March is not the warmest of places, but I survived and made plans.

The first shows in Canada were a series of one-night stands in Chilliwack, Mission City, Abbotsford, Hope, and Trail, B.C. A friendly printer supplied me with some posters, and we gave complimentary passes to all of the storekeepers in each town who displayed a poster. Although the first shows were full on account of the free tickets, we made barely enough money to pay the hall rentals. I told each of my audiences that I was returning ten days later with a completely changed show. The tactics worked, and word-of-mouth advertising gave us packed houses at each return and enabled us to return again for a third time.

By the end of April I was able to move from the cottage into a hotel with clean sheets and central heating. It felt like the height of luxury. I was able to send money to Coral, and could foresee a bright future.

At about that time I was befriended by the young advertising manager of the Chilliwack *Progress*, David Moyer, and one day over a golf game he came up with a public relations coup that was to open doors all over British Columbia. I told David how I had been approached in Honolulu by the pro at the Wailaie Golf Club, a man named Anthony. He had a young executive with him who was taking lessons and who suffered from nervous headaches. And Anthony's own game was suffering on account of the social pressures of his occupation. Could I, Anthony wondered, improve both of their games? Each had proven an excellent subject for the superconscious state. Anthony's game returned to his former high standard. The student's game did not improve, since he lacked the developed skills to make this possible; but his headaches stopped.

David reminded me that he had been a successful subject on stage, and suggested that I invite the paper's sports editor out to the golf course for an experiment.

Golfers, like many other sportsmen, often reach a plateau beyond which they seem unable to rise. In David's case, he had never been able to score better than 100 strokes on an eighteen-hole course. I gave him the appropriate superconscious suggestions to improve his game, and he played a round in front of several witnesses: sports editor George Inglis, local businessman Ted Germique, and some radio reporters. David completed the course in 84! From then on I presented a similar demonstration in almost every city we played, and the resultant publicity helped pack theaters. The average reduction in players' scores as a result of superconscious suggestion was 10 strokes, and the largest 16.

Ted and Audrienne Lovo of Rosedale, B.C., joined the show, and we moved into the Okanagan valley for the summer. Then in Osoyoos I met Tom and Roz Barton. Tom had a great interest in the potential of the human mind, and also happened to be an Immigration officer. I made a clean breast of my present status, and Tom immediately contacted his superiors. They agreed with him that I should be granted landed immigrant status. By the end of summer I was able to bring Coral and our three boys to join me. I also sent for my Australian advance man, Bill Harwood. Finally, we were really on our way.

I had promised myself, during that dreary bus ride to Vancouver, that I would take the show to the top within a year. By the anniversary of my arrival, March 16, 1962, I had played four straight weeks in Calgary's largest theater and two weeks each in Regina and Saskatoon, and was into my second week in Edmonton. Immediately ahead was my still-unequalled record of eight straight weeks at Vancouver's 2800-seat Orpheum Theater, and the birth of our fourth son in that same city in July. And the rest, as they say in the theater, is history.

That is about as autobiographical as I wish to get at this stage of my career. Perhaps in ten or twelve years the time will be right for the full autobiography that I certainly intend to write — some time.

Before concluding let me answer the question I am most often asked, namely: what was the funniest show so far in my career? Without doubt it was the opening night at the Pavillion Theater in Bournemouth, England, in 1982. There was a morticians' convention in town, and 168 of the conventioneers bought tickets for the show. About half of the 168 volunteered to come on stage. One does not usually associate morticians with humor; but I assure you, if I had been able to hire every top comedian in the world, the show could not have been funnier. If I had only videotaped that show, I might have had the top-selling comedy video ever.

As for retirement: Why should I retire? A person retires from a job or profession that he finds arduous in order to relax and engage in something he likes better. I love the theater and the pleasure that I bring to thousands each year as an entertainer. For that reason I will never retire as long as there is a demand for my particular talent. And it is a source of great satisfaction that I am now playing to the children and grandchildren of my original audiences of the 1960s — as well as to the grandparents who continue to come back year after year. Playing to repeat audiences means that I am continually competing with myself, and must therefore try to be sharper and better than last year. Oh well, I always did love a challenge!

NOTES

CHAPTER ONE

1 Ian Wilson, *Mind Out of Time*, London, p. 65.
2 S.J. Van Pelt, *Hypnotism and the Power Within*, 1955 edition, London, charts facing pp. 161, 176.
3 Morton Schatzman, *The Story of Ruth*, London, 1980.
4 Wilson, *op. cit.*, pp. 244-245.
5 A.R. Owen, *Hysteria, Hypnosis and Healing*, London, 1971, pp. 178-181.
6 For an up-to-date report on the use of hypnosis as an anesthesia in surgery, see 'Hypnotism Under the Knife', by Joanne Silberner, in *Science News*, 129 (March 22, 1986), pp. 186-187.

CHAPTER TWO

1 William Sargant, *The Battle for the Mind*, London, 1970.
2 Franz Hartmann, *The Life of Paracelsus*, London, 1887, p. 4.
3 *ibid*, p. 11.
4 *ibid*, p. 134.
5 *ibid*, p. 119.
6 *ibid*, p. 137.
7 *ibid*, p. 141.
8 A.R.G. Owen, *Hysteria, Hypnosis and Healing*, London, 1971, p. 171.
9 Anton Mesmer, *Mesmerism*, tr. G. Frankau, London, 1948, pp. 34-5, 42.
10 D.M. Walmsley, *Anton Mesmer*, London, 1967, p. 9.
11 *ibid*, p. 32.

Chapter Two (continued)

12 *ibid*, p. 52.
13 *ibid*.
14 *ibid*.
15 *ibid*, p. 54.
16 Anton Mesmer, *op. cit.*, pp. 37-39.
17 *ibid*, p. 32.
18 *ibid*, p. 33.
19 Anton Mesmer, *Memoir of F.A. Mesmer, 1799*, tr. J. Eden, Mt Vernon, NY, 1957, pp. 4, 14.
20 *ibid*, p. 24.
21 *ibid*, p. 36.
22 *ibid*, pp. 32-33.
23 *ibid*, pp. 34, 48.
24 *ibid*, p. 43.
25 Mesmer, 1948, p. 43.
26 Walmsley, *op. cit.*, pp. 79-80.
27 *ibid*, p. 65.
28 *ibid*, pp. 113, 115.
29 *ibid*, p. 155.

CHAPTER THREE

1 S.J. Van Pelt, *Hypnotism and the Power Within*, London, 1955, p. 127.
2 *ibid*, p. 178.
3 K. Ellis, *Science and the Supernatural*, London, 1974, pp. 146-147. Van Pelt, *op. cit.*, pp. 127-128.
4 Ellis, *op. cit.*, p. 146.
5 *ibid*, p. 151.
6 *New World Translation of the Holy Scriptures*, Brooklyn, NY, 1981.
7 Van Pelt, *op. cit.*, p. 185.
8 M.L. Gross, *The Psychological Society*, NY, 1978, pp. 246, 244, 242, 241, 238, 237, 243. See also F. Crews' *Skeptical Engagements*, Oxford U.P., NY, 1986.
9 *Lancet*, May 26, 1984.
10 Martin Gardner, *Fads and Fallacies in the Name of Science*, NY, 1958, pp. 187-201.

CHAPTER FOUR

[1] K. Ellis, *Science and the Supernatural*, 1974, p. 124.
[2] *ibid*, pp. 124-125.
[3] V. Buranelli, *The Wizard From Vienna*, London, 1976, p. 100.
[4] *ibid*, p. 208.
[5] *ibid*.
[6] R.W. Marks, *The Story of Hypnotism*, p. 75.
[7] J.M. Bramwell, *Hypnotism: Its History, Practice and Theory*, London, 1960, p. 9.
[8] *ibid*, p. 10.
[9] Marks, *op. cit.*, p. 74.
[10] J. Esdaile, *The Introduction of Mesmerism into the Public Hospitals of India*, London, 1856, p. 22.
[11] F.L. Marcuse, *Hypnotism: Fact and Fiction*, Penguin Books, 1959, pp. 48-49.
[12] Bramwell, *op. cit.*, p. 20.
[13] *ibid*, p. 19.
[14] Esdaile, *op. cit.*, p. 40.
[15] J.L. Orton, *Emile Coué: The Man and his Work*, London, 1935, p. 68.
[16] *ibid*, p. 79.

CHAPTER FIVE

[1] Morey Bernstein, *The Search for Bridey Murphy*, NY, 1956, pp. 7-8.
[2] *ibid*, pp. 9, 10, 112, 114.
[3] C.D. MacDougall, *Superstition and the Press*, Buffalo, 1984.
[4] Jeffrey Iverson, *More Lives Than One?*, London, 1977.
[5] *ibid*, p. 52.
[6] *Free Inquiry*, Fall 1986, p. 23.
[7] *Skeptical Inquirer*, Winter 1985/86, p. 99; *Free Inquiry*, Fall 1986, pp. 18-23.
[8] *Free Inquiry*, Fall 1986, p. 22.
[9] Ian Wilson, *Mind Out of Time*, London, 1981, p. 101.
[10] *ibid*, p. 100.
[11] *ibid*, p. 126.
[12] *ibid*, p. 60.
[13] Helen Wambach, *Reliving Past Lives: The Evidence Under Hypnosis*,

Chapter Five (continued)

London, 1979; H & D Arnall Bloxham, *Reincarnation: Myth or Fact? Research into Reincarnation*, London, 1982; Ian Stevenson, *Twenty Cases Suggestive of Reincarnation*, Virginia University Press, 1974.
[14] Ian Wilson, *op. cit.*, p. 100.
[15] *ibid*, p. 110.
[16] Robert A. Baker, "The Effect of Suggestion on Past-Lives Regression," *American Journal of Clinical Hypnosis*, 25(1), July 1982, pp.71-76.

CHAPTER SIX

[1] M. Netherton & N. Shiffrin, *Past Lives Therapy*, NY, 1978, pp. 47-55.
[2] *ibid*, pp. 78-85.
[3] *ibid*, pp. 16-17.
[4] Ian Wilson, *Mind Out of Time*, London, 1981, pp. 249-251.
[5] *Free Inquiry*, Spring 1987, p. 55
[6] *Time*, December 15, 1986, p. 36.
[7] *Newsweek*, December 15, 1986, p. 42.
[8] Wilson, *op. cit.*, p. 246.
[9] *ibid*.
[10] For additional information on this point, see the 'Mail' section of *Abra Cadabra*, vol. 82, # 2123, Oct. 4, 1986, p. 356, and additional letters in the following issues.
[11] James Randi, *The Truth About Uri Geller*, Buffalo, NY, 1984.
[12] David Marks and Richard Kammann, *The Psychology of the Psychic*, Buffalo, NY, 1980.
[13] James Randi, 'Project Alpha: Part 1,' *Skeptical Inquirer*, Summer, 1983, vol. 7, # 4; 'Project Alpha: Part 2,' *Skeptical Inquirer*, Fall, 1983, vol. 8, #1.
[14] For an interpretation of such thought processes, see Paul Kurtz's *The Transcendental Temptation*, Buffalo, NY, 1986.
[15] Very few of Philip Magonet's journal articles were ever rewritten into books. About the only book that is readily available to the general public in North America is his *Practical Hypnotism*, No. Hollywood, 1976.
[16] Doctors will have no trouble finding Kroger's articles through the indices of the main medical journals. For the general public, the most readily obtainable book by William Kroger is *Childbirth With Hypnosis*, Hollywood, 1965.

Chapter Six (continued)

[17] Herbert Spiegel and David Spiegel, *Trance and Treatment: Clinical Uses of Hypnosis*, NY, 1978.

INDEX

acupuncture, 50-51
age regression, 71, 94
amnesia, 54, 59, 67
anesthesia, 8, 16-17, 62-64, 66-67
Asklepios, 18
astrology, 26, 37, 97, 99
Atkins, Sue, 84
"aura", 60

Baker, Robert, 85-86
Basil, R., 97
Bernheim, Dr., 47-48, 58, 68
Bernstein, Morey, 70-73, 79
Bertrand, Alexandre, 57-60
Bloxham, Arnall, 75-79, 82-83
Braddon, Russell, 40
Braid, James, 12, 58, 60-61, 65-68, 106
"Bridey Murphy", 71-74, 79
Breuer, Dr., 46
Burkmar, Lucius, 39

Carson, Johnny, 100
Cayce, Edgar, 55-56, 102
"channeling", 97-98
Charcot, Dr., 47, 68
Charles, Prince, 84

Chenevix, Richard, 61
Christian Science, 38-41, 51
clairvoyance, 39, 55, 61, 64-65
Clawson, Thomas, 106-107
cognitive dissonance, 104
Committee for the Scientific Investigation of Claims of the Paranormal, 101
Constain, C.B., 78
Coué, Emile, 68-69, 96, 106

delayed superconscious reaction, 57, 60
Deleuze, J.F., 60
De Wohl, Louis, 76-78
dianetics, 50
Dixon, Jeane, 93, 100
doublethink, 105
Doyle, Conan, 38
"druid sleep", 18
Dumas, Alexandre, 58
Dupotet, Baron, 61

Eddy, Mary Baker, 38-41
electro-shock therapy, 29
Elliotson, John, 16, 60-64
Erickson, Milton, 107

— 131 —

Esdaile, James, 16-17, 60, 63-65
extra-sensory perception, 52, 55, 61, 65, 99-102
Eysenck, Hans, 84

faithhealing, 33, 35, 51
fakirs, Indian, 98, 118
Faria, Abbe, 56-59, 61
Fenwick, Peter, 15
flying saucers, 99, 105
Fox sisters, 38
Freud, Sigmund, 45-49, 68

Gassner, Father, 33
Gauquelin, Michel, 37
Geller, Uri, 2, 100-102
genetic memory theory, 87-88
ghosts, 15-16
Gross, M.L., 45-46
Guerineau, Dr., 16

Hartley, Brian, 76
Hartmann, Franz, 23-24
Hell, Maximilian, 22, 25-26, 29
Hill, Barney, 105
homeopathy, 50-51
Hope, Bob, 72
Houdini, Harry, 2, 36-38, 98
Hubbard, Ron, 50-51
Hurkos, Peter, 100
Hurst, Harry, 79
hypnotism myths, 5-9, 11, 43-44, 59

Ingenhousze, Dr., 30-31
Iverson, Jeffrey, 75, 78
"Jane Evans", 75-79
Jehovah's Witnesses, 41-42

Keeton, Joe, 82-84
Knight, J.Z., 97
Kolough, F., 108
Kreskin, 100-101

Kroger, Dr., 107

Liebeault, Dr., 47, 58, 68

Magonet, Philip, 106
Maharishi Mahishi Yogi, 3-4, 98
Marie Antoinette, 34
Marks, Dr. David, 94-95, 101
medical hypnotists, 42-45
memory enhancement, 94-96, 105
Mesmer, Anton, 22-37, 52-53, 58, 98
Mozart, L. and W., 27, 29
multiple personality, 21-22, 97

National Inquirer, 100
naturopathy, 50-51
Netherton, M., 90
N-rays, 31

obstetrics, 107
Oesterling, Franzl, 27-29
Okey, Elizabeth, 62
Orwell, George, 105
Oscan language, 79-80, 94, 102
osteopathy, 50-51
Oudet, Dr., 16
Owen, A.R., 25

Packard, Vance, 13
palmistry, 99
Paracelsus, 22-25
parapsychology, 52, 100-102
past-life regression, 70-88, 93, 105
past-lives therapy, 7, 85-94
phrenology, 61, 67, 99
Pius VI, Pope, 33
Pollock, John, 91-93
"possession", 18-21, 33, 90, 96-97
Poyen, Charles, 39
premonitions, 102-103
Project Alpha, 101-102

Proudfoot, Wilf, 91
"psychic archaeology", 99
"psychic prophecy", 61-62, 93, 100-103
"psychic surgery", 51
psychoanalysis, 45-51
Puysegur, Marquis de, 53-56, 59

Walmsley, D.M., 26
Wambach, Helen, 82-83
"watchdog", 7-10, 12, 20, 54, 68, 73, 96, 103-104
Wiggin, James, 40
Wilson, Ian, 14, 15, 84, 91-92
witchcraft, 20-21, 97

Quimby, Phineas, 38-40, 55-56

Randi, James, 2, 101
Raschke, Carl, 97
reincarnation theory, 7, 70-88, 97
Robbins, Harold, 99
Rosen, Harold, 79-80
Russell, Charles, 41-42
"Ruth", 15-16

Sargant, William, 21
Schatzman, Morton, 15
scientology, 50-51
seance, 36-38, 56, 62
Shaw, Steven, 99
Skinner, B.F., 21
smoking habit, 104
Spiegel, H. and D., 107
spiritualism, 36-38, 56, 61, 97-98
Stern, Dr. Bernard, 107
Stevenson, Ian, 81-83
subliminal advertising, 13
superconscious reasoning, 103

television, hypnotism in, 5-6, 43, 59, 74-75, 78, 80, 108
Tighe, Virginia, 71-74
trance theory, 11-13, 68
UFOs, 99, 105

Van Pelt, S.J., 14, 38, 43, 49-50, 106
Velikovsky, I., 99
Von Daniken, Erich, 99